TEACHINGS OF NATURE

I.H.W.

Hungry Wolf, Adolf.
  Teachings of nature / Adolf Hungry Wolf ; with drawings of Iniskim and Okan Hungry Wolf.
     p. cm.
  Reprint. Originally published: Invermere, B.C. : Good Medicine Books, c1975. (Good Medicine Book ; no. 14)
  Includes bibliographical references.
  ISBN 0-913990-75-2 : $8.95
  1. Indians of North America. 2. Ethnobotany—North America. 3. Ethnozoology—North America. I. Title.
E98.B7H86 1991
  970.004'97—dc20   91-17795
                      CIP

ISBN 0-913990-75-2

Book Publishing Company
PO Box 99
Summertown, TN 38483 USA

Canadian ISBN 0-920698-27-1

Published in Canada by
Good Medicine Books
Box 844
Skookumchuck, B.C. Canada V0B 2E0

Design and Paste-up -- Adolf Hungry Wolf
Typing -- Lea Priore

Parts of this book were originally published as "Teachings of Nature", No. 14 in the Good Medicine Cultural Handbook series, 1975.

TEACHINGS OF NATURE

Adolf Hungry Wolf

with Drawings by Iniskim and Okan Hungry Wolf

**Book Publishing
Company
Summertown, TN
USA**

**Good
Medicine
Books
Skookumchuck, B.C.
Canada**

CONTENTS

INTRODUCTION

Growing concerns about our Environment are causing many people to learn more about the Nature that is around them. "Life in Harmony with Nature" is no longer just a motto from an outdated social movement. It is becoming a major theme among world leaders, who recognize that with out it we may not have a World for the 21st Century.

North America's original people lived in harmony with nature for ages, until Europeans came and brought newer ways, based more on the clever skills of men and women than on the variable offerings of nature. Life became easier, things were more plentiful, for a long time it seemed everything was working out well. Most people thought the "old ways" described in this book belonged only to the primitive past.

This book is certainly not meant to promote a "return to the old ways." The modern world has changed too much for that to be a practical alternative. We can no longer live from hunting and fishing alone; most of today's complicated diseases cannot be cured simply by brewing up a pot of wild plants; appointments and deadlines cannot be met just by keeping time with the Sun, Moon, and Stars.

Yet, some of the knowledge in this book can still be of direct use for those who want to put it into practice. But more importantly, it will help us to understand how the native people of the past lived with respect and reverence for nature. Perhaps that understanding will inspire us to work harder in this new world effort at restoring balance between human-kind and Nature.

NATIVE USES OF WILD PLANTS

Food and medicine are the two most important native uses for wild plants; many people today still gather them for that. Other uses include the making of baskets, boats, tools, lodges and even traditional clothing. Some plants served as dyes, shampoos, perfumes, smoking mixtures and ceremonial incense. Littering caused no long term ecological problems in the past because everything the native people had, turned back into the nature that it came from.

Roots and berries were always the most important food plants, because they could be gathered in great quantities and preserved for easy storage. Roots were mostly dug in the Spring, when they are tender, while berries were gathered through the Summer, as they became ripe.

Several kinds of containers were made and used for gathering and storing wild plants. Baskets were most popular in the Southwest and along the Pacific Coast; some were large enough to hide a small child. Bags made by weaving grasses or corn husk strands were especially popular among the Plateau tribes. People in the East often preferred birchbark containers, some made like large boxes with lids. Buffalo hunters of the Plains pre ferred rawhide bags for storing their food supplies.

A typical rawhide bag was of one piece, perhaps a foot wide and three feet long. The hide was scraped clean of fat, tissue and hair. Then it was folded, lengthwise, and the two sides were laced up with strips of rawhide. The fold was made so that one piece was longer. The extra piece on the longer side was folded again, to make a flap. While the hide was still wet, it was stuffed with grass, leaves or sand. When it was dry, the stuffings were dumped out, leaving the rawhide bag shaped with a permanent bulge. Similar bags can be made with fully tanned leather, which will stretch when filled.

Another kind of gathering bag was often made from the bark of cedar and birch trees - sometimes even young fir trees. A typical one of these was made by the Flathead people of western Montana. Its shape tapered from a round top to a pointed, rectangular bottom. It measured about a foot in diameter and about two feet or less in height. It was made from a rectangular slab of bark about twice the length of the final container. The bark was folded in half and two cuts, about two inches long, were made from each edge of the fold toward the centre. The bark was then bent into a cylindrical shape, and the seams were trimmed and fitted until they overlapped each other about an inch. The seams were then pierced and sewn together with strips of willow bark. At other times, they were pierced and then pinned together with small, green twigs. A willow hoop was sewn inside the top of the basket to make it circular. The seams on the inside of it were then smeared with pitch, to make them waterproof.

Another kind of storage bag was popular with tribes who lived near the Rocky Mountains. It was made from pieces of elk, deer or moose hide, sections from two extremities being used. One variation was the "Foot Bag", made by skinning out two or more feet, from the knee to the hoof, then sewing these pieces together to make a bag. A round piece of tanned leather was usually sewn on to make a bottom. Another piece of leather was hemmed to the top. With a drawstring through it, this top piece closes the bag tightly.

The other variation was made by sewing two or more skinned heads together. A head bag was often made quite large - two or three moose heads sewn together. The noses were trimmed off. Bottoms were made with round pieces of leather or rawhide, like the foot bags. The necks formed the tops, and these were closed with buckskin thongs.

Women of the past often had several such skin bags in which they kept separate their collections of berries, roots, fats and dried meats. The put bunches of wild mint into the bags to flavour the contents and to help with their preservation. Flies and bugs generally don't like wild mint.

Kids in the tribal days had no cookie jars, but they often raided these storage bags for treats. Grandmothers were especially vulnerable, since they always had a good supply of things that grandkids like. Winter-time guests were sometimes treated to assorted dried foods from these bags. The food would be eaten raw, or speared on a green, sharpened stick and roasted over the fire.

5

DYES

The Southwest desert people probably knew more about plants to use for dying than anyone else, since they spent much time weaving their fine rugs and other products. Here is how they got some of their colours.

Black: Sumac (Rhus trilobata) bark was boiled for about two hours with another ingredient. Among the Zuni this was a certain clay that contained sulphate of iron, aluminium, and magnesium. Among the Navajo it was a yellow earth paint mixed with pinyon gum. Blue: The black-seeded sunflower gave a purplish blue. The dark navy bean from the garden gave a dark blue. A light blue was made from the larkspur plant (Delphinium). Indigo was obtained from Mexico and dissolved in children's urine. The solution was boiled with black to make darker shades of blue. Purple: Obtained from the seeds of the cultivated sunflower and of purple corn. Red: A certain grass (Thelesperma gracile) gave a brownish red. Purple corn gave a pinkish red, if properly diluted. Pigweed (Amara nthus retroflexus) gave a pink. Real red was not produced until the people obtained scarlet cloth from Spaniards and traders. These they unravelled and boiled. Yellow: The flowers of rabbit brush (Crysothamnus bigelovi) gave a bright yellow. Green: The article was dyed yellow first, then soaked for a short time in the blue dye. White: A sandy clay containing gypsum was mixed with warm water.

Some people even dyed their leathers a rich reddish brown colour with the roots of the mountain mahogany, which is found in the Southwest.

In the Northern lands, other plants were available for dyes. The Flathead people boiled the bark of alder trees (Alnus icana) to make a bright dye which they sometimes used to make their hair a weird orange colour. A few of the people kept up this practice until fairly recently. The Blackfoot people used the owl clover to make a red dye for feathers and other decorations.

Other Blackfoot dyes included violet flowers, which made blue, some kinds of lichens, which produced green, and the roots of the oregon grape, which made a mellow yellow.

PERFUMES

Sweet grass was the favourite perfume of most native people. They used it for incense, they packed it with their clothes,they boiled it for use as a hair wash. It grows in moist places all over the land. Often you can find it by its scent, which carries a long ways. It will grow several feet tall, if livestock doesn't come around to trim it.

Meadow Rue (Thalictrum species) was another popular perfume. The whole plant could be used, but ideally the seeds were stripped off and dried. Most of the odour is contained by them. This plant served as an insect repellent, as well. It was used to keep bugs out of clothing. For personal perfume the seeds were chewed until pulverized, then rubbed over the body and through the hair.

Yarrow (Achillea millefolium) flowers when fresh, were used as an underarm deodorant.

Sage (Artemisia species) was crushed and rubbed on the body as a deodorant. It was also used to counter bad smells in clothing, moccasins, and other parts of the body.

SHAMPOOS

The favourite shampoos were suds made from yucca roots, for those who could find the plant.

Orange Honeysuckle (Lonicera cilosa), a climbing vine, was boiled to make a shampoo by the Flathead people. They said it made their hair grow longer.

Another Flathead shampoo was made by boiling virgin's bower (Clema sOtis columbiana) together with pine drops (Pterospora andromedea), which is a tall straight plant that grows in moist, wooded areas.

Still another shampoo was made by boiling a certain weed (Verbascum sOblattaria) that belongs to the figwort family. They say this shampoo lathered like soap. It turned the hair somewhat darker and made it grow longer. More of the plant was needed if it was used dry.

BEADS

Beads used to be made from bones, pieces of stone, plus various seeds and berries, including silver berries, rose hips and juniper berries. Such beads were used to decorate buckskin clothing before glass beads were introduced by traders from Europe. Berries were often strung up for necklaces and wristlets.

There was an old way of decorating berries that were to be used as beads. A fire was made with dry wood on which grease was dropped. The necklaces and strung-up beads were held in the greasy smoke until they were covered by a layer of dark grease. They were then rubbed and polished with a soft piece of buckskin until they had a dark, shiny finish.

WILD PLANTS TO EAT

ACORNS Although the many tribes of California had numerous wild plants available for eating, their staple food was the acorn. Lifestyles and tribal economies were based around the acorn harvest, which came once a year. Everyone took part, men and boys climbing trees to knock the acorns down, women and children gathering them into large baskets for storage and processing.

Hulling was the first step in preparing acorns. Seeds were placed on end into shallow grooves cut into stones, where they were pressed with other stones until the kernels were released. The gathered kernels were then pounded on a flat stone until it turned into a medium-grained meal.

The bitter and poisonous tannic acid was then removed by spreading this meal out in a shallow pit and pouring containers of hot water over it until, by taste, it was found to have lost its bitterness. It was left to dry, then broken up into chunks that were later baked into bread or boiled into a mush.

ARROWHEAD *(Sagittaria latifolia)*

This plant gets its name from the shape of its large leaves. It has white flowers and grows to about three feet high in shallow waters.

Arrowhead roots were eaten by many tribes. They look like tiny potatoes, varying in size from a pea to an egg. They are best in Summer, but can also be eaten in Winter if they are not frozen. The plants were loosened with a stick, or with bare feet, after which they float to the surface. They were eaten raw, boiled, or roasted on a bed of coals. To prepare them for storage, they were boiled, sliced, then put out to dry.

BALSAM ROOT *(Balsamorrhiza species)*

Better known by the name Sunflower, its seeds were a popular snack, eaten raw or pounded into meal. In the Spring the flowering stems are tender and can be eaten raw after being peeled. The long, fleshy roots were dug, peeled, then baked in a pit, like camas. The Flathead people baked these roots for at least three days in order to soften the tough fibres, after which they say it tastes like sweet potato.

BEARBERRY *(Arctostaphylos uva-ursi)*

This low-growing shrub is also known as manzanita and kinnikinnick, the latter being a native name for smoking mix, which was the most important use for the shiny green leaves.

Bearberries can be eaten raw any time after they ripen and turn red, usually in August. Their mealy taste is not particularly exciting, but since they stay on the plants all Winter, they can make an important emergency food. With more time for preparation, the berries' flat taste can be improved by mixing them with grease, then frying them until they begin to split open.

The Flathead people used to predict their Winters by looking at bear berry bushes. If there were few berries, they expected a mild Winter; many berries usually meant Winter would be tough.

BITTERROOT *(Lewisia rediviva and pygmaea)*

A very popular plant of the Rocky Mountain region, used as a trade article by tribes whose country had quantities, such as the Flathead-Salish people and the Kootenays.

Bitterroots were dug as soon as they began to flower, sometime in May. Once the plant is in full bloom, its edible root is thought to be past its prime; after the blooms have fallen, it was not dug any more at all. As soon as each root was dug up, its top was twisted off and discarded. Some people also cut out the heart, or inner core, which causes most of the bitter taste. Back in camp, the roots were peeled and washed right away.

CAMAS *(Camassia quamash)*

One of the most popular wild plant foods, camas is found in moist meadows near the Rocky Mountain regions. Its stem and leaves rise up one to two feet from an underground bulb, which is dug up in the Fall, after the blue flowers have fallen off. By this time black seeds will have formed inside the pods.

Many tribes had favourite camas grounds where they moved in the Fall just for harvesting. Although camas bulbs grow larger in some places than in others, native harvesters were more interested in finding sweet-tasting bulbs than searching for size. The Flatheads, for instance, preferred camas found in the area of Camas Hot Springs, Montana, over ones that grew closer to their traditional camping places.

Fresh camas bulbs were often just boiled and eaten. However, the more common method of preparation was to bake them in special pits. A typical pit was a four by six foot rectangle, about two feet deep. It was filled with good firewood, which was covered by a layer of stones. Some used small river rocks, while others preferred flat stones from the prairies. Either way, the wood was allowed to burn until it turned to ashes, leaving the pit lined with red-hot stones. These were then covered with a layer of green grass or green wood, topped by fresh branches and leaves, making a mat several inches thick. The camas bulbs were then spread out on top of this mat, after their skins had been peeled off. The layer of bulbs was next covered with another layer of green grass, else a layer of black tree moss that had been soaked in water. Over this came another layer of slough grass, or more green twigs and leaves. Finally, the whole pit was covered with four to six inches of dirt, over which a fire was built and kept going for three days and nights, the length depending on the quantity of camas underneath.

When the pit was reopened, children liked to gather the small twigs and suck from them the sweet juices of the roasted bulbs. These bulbs could be eaten right away, though most of them were dried in the Sun and packed away for Winter storage. They could be dried whole, else mashed with a stone pestle and formed into round cakes. Meat grinders later replaced stone pestles. Berries were often mixed with the camas bulb mash, before it was dried.

Roasted camas bulbs are said to be sweeter than raw ones, with a taste similar to roasted chestnuts. The Flathead people used the brew from boiled camas bulbs to make a sweet, hot drink similar to coffee. They also made a thick gravy by cooking the baked bulbs with flour and water.

CATTAIL *(Typha latifolia)*

This common marsh plant is easily identified by its dark brown, fuzzy spike. The fuzz burns very readily and makes good tinder for starting campfires. Cattail pollen can be eaten raw, else ground into a flour from which the people of some tribes made a form of bread and cake. Others used it for insulation in their Winter moccasins.

Cattail roots can be cooked and roasted. First, they must be cleaned, peeled and defibered. They can then be boiled into a mush, or baked in a pit, like camas. They can also be dried and stored. The dried roots were ground into a meal with a stone pestle, then mixed into other foods.

CHOKECHERRY *(Prunus virginana)*

Also known as "wild cherry", these small, purple fruits grow on tall bushes, ripening in early Fall. They are not good to eat unripe; most people say they should not be gathered until after the first frost. Freezing improves their flavour and makes them sweeter.

Fresh chokecherries are boiled with water and fat, then sweetened to make a kind of soup. If the small stones are swallowed whole, they tend to gather and cause constipation. For that reason, chokecherries were usually crushed; they taste better that way, too. They are placed on a flat rock, a few at a time, then pounded with a rounded stone or pestle until the pits are completely pulverized, resembling finely-ground coffee.

The crushed chokecherries are then formed into small cakes, like cookies, then placed into Sunlight to dry. Usually the cakes were placed on a framework of small sticks and turned frequently to keep them from spoiling on their damp side. Chokecherries were often mixed with other berries before being crushed and dried. In more recent times they have been crushed through meat grinders rather than with stones.

Preparing chokecherries properly is quite an art. If they're not crushed well, they are hard to eat because of the stones. Grease is mixed with the small cakes to keep them from drying out too hard.

Popular storage bags for chokecherries were made from the whole skins of small animals. Wild mint was stuffed into the animal's legs to keep the cherries from falling out while still allowing some air to get into the bag, keeping its contents from becoming mouldy.

Pemmican was commonly made with chokecherries. First, cakes of dried cherries were broken up into a bowl of water and allowed to soak. When the cherries had become soft, the water was strained out. This resulted in a popular drink known as Chokecherry Brew. The soaked cherries were then mixed with fat; most popular was backfat, which did not cake up so easily. Bacon drippings have become a common substitute. The fat and cherry mixture must be pounded together really well, then kneaded into small balls. These were eaten fresh, else placed into special rawhide containers to be taken along on hunting trips or war raids. Sometimes this greasy, kneaded mixture was formed into brick-like cakes, then sewn up inside a rawhide covering, somewhat like cheese, for later use.

Stems of chokecherry wood have many traditional uses. Being a hard wood, it works good for pipe stems, tipi pegs, bows and arrows. Even if dry chokecherry wood is lying on the ground it will not soak up water, so it makes good emergency firewood, especially in rain or snow. Thin, fresh sticks of the wood were often stuck into meat roasts as a flavouring. A tea can also be made from the bark scrapings.

COW PARSNIP *(Heracleum lanatum)*

A sturdy plant that grows up to ten feet tall and has large leaves; sometimes known as "wild rhubarb". The young stalks can be peeled and eaten raw. They can also be cut up, like celery, and boiled. Be careful not to confuse the young stalks with those of the poisonous hemlock plants.

Cow parsnip roots were cut up and dried for Winter use, sometimes being dipped in blood first, for extra flavouring. The dried roots were boiled and sweetened for eating.

Mature cow parsnip stalks become pithy, which made them suitable for use as deer and elk calls, being fitted with a reeded mouthpiece for the purpose.

DANDELION *(Tarasum species)*

The common dandelion's young leaves make a tender vegetable early in the season. They may be eaten raw, in salads, or boiled. As they mature, they must be boiled longer, or in several changes of water, to avoid their bitter taste. It is said that dandelions contain twenty-five times more vitamin A than tomato juice.

INDIAN BREADROOT *(Psoralea esculenta)*

This is the "wild turnip" used by most tribes of the Plains to supplement their main food of buffalo meat. The plant grows in abundance throughout the Great Plains and other regions.

Wild turnip roots were dug shortly before the flowers dropped from the plant. They were peeled and eaten raw, else roasted over an open fire or in a bed of coals. Mostly they were peeled and strung up in quantity to dry beneath the Sun, after which they were easy to store. Some coated the peeled and dried roots with fat to keep them from becoming too hard during storage.

LABRADOR TEA *(Ledum groenlandicum)*

A low-growing, sweet-smelling shrub that provided a healthy drink for the people of many tribes. Several species of this plant grow in moist and cool areas, usually at higher altitudes. In former times, families often dried several pounds of the leaves for Winter use.

To make Labrador Tea, steep a few of the leaves in boiling water. Change the water once or twice for a mild tea, or let the leaves soak in the water overnight if you want strong tea with much flavour. Strength of the tea can be judged by its colour; greenish for weak tea, deep red for very strong.

LAMB'S QUARTERS *(Chenopodium album)*

he young leaves of this plant, also known as pigweed, have been compared to cabbage and spinach. They were often prepared in the same way. They can also be eaten fresh, as a salad. The plants bear many black seeds, which can be boiled into porridge, else ground into a meal which can be baked into cakes.

LODGEPOLE PINE *(Pinas contorta)*

This is the preferred wood for tipi poles, which the people of many tribes replaced every year. During the peeling process, workers often ate sparingly of the sap. The juicy inner bark (the cambium layer) was eaten fresh, or dried for later use. It also served as an emergency food. Children liked the semi-hard red bubbles of pitch on the bark, which they chewed like gum.

MARIPOSA LILY *(Calochortus species)*

A common flowering plant whose base is formed by a bulb about the size of a walnut. These bulbs can be boiled, roasted, or steamed in quantity inside of pits, like camas.

ROSEBERRY *(Rosa acicularis and others)*

A common bush in most areas, also known as wild rose and rose hips. They are usually gathered after the first frost, but also served as an important emergency food, since they stay on the bushes through Winter.

An excellent source of vitamin C, these berries can be eaten fresh, or else prepared in several ways. Roseberry meal was made by boiling fresh rose hips, then crushing them together with fat and cooking the mixture over a fire (usually in a frying pan, or "black plate", as they were known in some native languages). The fried meal was then sweetened and eaten. Fresh berries were also mixed with flour, sweetened, then boiled into a porridge. Sometimes they were used in place of other berries for making pemmican.

A ball of cooked roseberries mixed with fat was one of the first solid foods fed to many Indian babies. Roseberry soup was considered good food for growing children. The berries are easily dried and stored.

SASKATOON BERRY *(genus Amelanchier, which has dozens of species)*

The most important berry for many tribes, it is also known as serviceberry or juneberry, while in the Blackfoot language it is the "real berry".

Saskatoon berries usually ripen in mid-Summer, about the time that many tribes gather traditionally for their annual encampments and ceremonials. Kids in these camps are often seen with purple mouths, usually learning the hard way that too many fresh berries will result in stomach aches and diarrhoea.

Spread on hides or pieces of canvas and left in the Sun for a couple of days, saskatoon berries dry easily, after which they can be stored for a long time to be used as sweetening for other foods. They were a common ingredient for pemmican, made by combining dried berries and ground-up dried meat with melted grease.

A popular ceremonial meal among some tribes is saskatoon berry soup, made either from fresh or dried berries. The berries are boiled in water, then mixed with flour for thickening and sugar for sweetening, along with pieces of bitterroot, meat or fat for extra flavour.

SKUNK CABBAGE *(Lysichiton americanum)*

This plant, with its large leaves, is commonly found in marshy places. The roots can be dried and ground into flour, which is said to have a very strong taste until after it has been stored for some time. The young leaves can be cooked as a fresh vegetable, changing the water several times to remove its strong taste. The roots can also be roasted in pits, like camas.

SPRING BEAUTY *(Claytonia lanceolata)*

A common plant, also known as "Indian Potato". This was often the first fresh vegetable food eaten after Winter, the roots being dug as soon as the pinkish-white flowers began to bloom, usually in April. They are only good for a short time, so they were seldom dried for later use. Instead, they were prepared by washing, then boiling or roasting.

SQUAW ROOT *(Perideria gairdneri)*

Another important root in native diets, also known as the "wild carrot". The plant grows from one to three feet tall, has small, white flowers and small roots, which were usually dug around June and July. They were eaten raw or boiled, else dried for storage. Some people preferred to boil and mash them before letting them dry in small cakes.

THISTLE *(Cirsum species)*

This often-bothersome plant has fairly large roots which led some people to call it the "Indian Turnip". These roots were peeled, then roasted in a pit, leaving them with a fairly sweet taste. The young flowering stems were also peeled, then boiled into a tender vegetable resembling celery. Some species are slightly poisonous, so it helps to know which kind grows in your area.

WATERCRESS *(Nasturtium aquaticum)*

A common water plant with shiny, dark green leaves and white flowers. The leaves can be cooked like spinach, or added raw to salads and stews. The raw stalks can be eaten like celery.

WILD LICORICE *(Glycorrhiza lepidota)*

The long, fleshy roots of this common plant have a sweet taste, which made them popular either raw, else roasted in a bed of hot coals or ashes.

WILD MINT *(Mentha species)*

This plant can be found in damp places, often identified from a distance by its strong aroma. In addition to making a popular tea and a fresh vegetable, the leaves were often added to dried meat and berries, both as a flavouring and to help keep flies and bugs away.

WILD ONION *(Allium species)*

Varieties of this plant can be found in many regions, although sometimes it is confused with a similar plant which is poisonous. Wild onions can be gathered from early Spring until late Fall and eaten raw, else added to soups and stews for flavouring.

WILD PARSLEY *(Lomatium simplex and cous)*

An important root among many tribes, also known as the "Indian Carrot" or "Indian Turnip", it was dug in Spring, just after the yellow flowers have finished blooming.

The large roots of wild parsley grow deep, so that digging them without modern tools was hard work, mostly performed by women. For this, they used special, fire-hardened sticks, rounded at one end and sharpened at the other. The round end was placed against the stomach of the digger, a thick piece of rawhide placed in between for protection. Body weight then forced the sharp end down into the ground.

WILD RICE OF THE WATERS

Wild Rice is one of North America's most valuable natural crops, both in taste and for trading. It grows in lakes, ponds, and slow-flowing streams from Manitoba to New Brunswick, Massachusetts to Nebraska, and as far south as parts of Florida and Louisiana.

Botanists say Wild Rice has not yet reached the limits of its potential range. They think all continents have suitable conditions for its growing. It can easily be transplanted, preferring water that moves, with mucky or silty bottoms. Seeds can be obtained from suppliers in Manitoba and Wisconsin. The following are preferred conditions for its successful growth:

1. Water no deeper than two feet in early Summer.
2. Water that circulates slowly.
3. No heavy competition from other plants.
4. Open bottom soil that is not covered by aquatic plants, stones, or other obstructions. (Some sites have been cultivated with harrows before successful crops were raised.)
5. Sites should not be exposed to strong winds, waves, boat traffic, floating logs, frequent shade, or Summer dry-ups.

MENOMINI USE OF WILD RICE

It is said that among all the forest tribes, the Menomini were most intimately associated with wild rice. Their tribal name comes from "mino-min", which refers to this valuable plant. Tribal traditions tell how wild rice was a gift to the forefathers from "underneath beings". Every year Menomini camps were set up along the lakeshores for harvesting wild rice, starting about the middle of September.

Tribal laws forbid any rice to be harvested until appointed leaders decide it is ripe enough. After making this decision, the chief of each band performs a ceremony of sacrifices and offerings to ensure that his people have a good harvest.

A typical harvest party consists of a man to pole the canoe and two women to gather the rice. The man uses a long pole whose forked end he pushes against the underwater rice roots, which give more resistance than the surrounding mud. As they slowly move along, the women use a shorter pole to pull bunches of rice plants into the boat. These are then hit crosswise with a stick, causing the ripe grain to fall into the bottom of the boat. They take great care to do this work with respect and reverence, wasting as little of the rice as possible. They go back and forth through the rice beds in adjoining lines, until the canoe is well filled.

Back at camp the rice is shuffled by hand and foot to knock off its tiny, sharp spikes, after which the edible parts are packed into leather sacks, birchbark bags, or even blankets. Immediately afterwards, always on the same day, a ceremonial meal of thanksgiving is held by all the harvesting families, after which the crop is hulled and winnowed, then prepared for long-term storage. Properly cached, the rice is then good for up to two years.

CHIPPEWA SUGAR CAMP

Told by Nodinens, White Earth, Minn., 1907

Excerpt from: Densmore, Frances **CHIPPEWA CUSTOMS**

"When we got to the sugar bush we took the birch-bark dishes out of the storage and the women began tapping the trees. We had queer-shaped axes made of iron. Our sugar camp was always near Mille Lac, and the men cut holes in the ice, put something over their heads, and fished through the ice. There were plenty of big fish in those days, and the men speared them. My father had some wire, and he made fishhooks and tied them on basswood cord, and he got lots of pickerel that way. A food cache was always near the sugar camp. We opened that and had all kinds of nice food that we had stored in the fall. There were cedar-bark bags of rice and there were cranberries sewed in birch-bark makuks and long strings of dried potatoes and apples. Grandmother had charge of all this, and made the young girls do the work. As soon as the little creeks opened, the boys caught lots of small fish, and my sister and I carried them to the camp and dried them on a frame. My mother had two or three big brass kettles that she had bought from an English trader and a few tin pails from the American trader. She used these in making the sugar."

"We had plenty of birch-bark dishes, but the children ate mostly from the large shells that we got along the lake shore. We had sauce from the dried cranberries and blueberries sweetened with the new maple sugar. The women gathered the inside bark of the cedar. This can only be gotten in the spring, and we got plenty of it for making mats and bags."

"Toward the end of the sugar season there was a great deal of thick sirup called 'the last run of sap', and we had lots of fish that we had dried. This provided us with food during the time we were making our gardens."

NATURAL MEDICINES

In recent times many ancient herbal cures have been scientifically found to contain valuable healing substances. Others, however, appear to have worked only in combination with rituals that certain people learned through visions, dreams or from older practitioners called medicine men and women. These latter plants are of little use in modern life because they depend on the faith a patient has in the healer, situations of "mind over matter", which cannot easily be duplicated outside their tribal and religious environments.

Most modern day medicine men and women keep their knowledge private and their practice limited to close family and friends. A few share their abilities more publicly, though among them have been some imitators who brought disgrace to themselves, their people and their ways. For instance, some have claimed to possess cures for ailments and diseases that are largely the result of modern living, while most agree that natural medicines are only effective for natural ailments. In any case, keep in mind that there is no medicine strong enough to prevent death when one's time has come for it.

The following lists of natural medicines are mostly those that any skilfull native person would have known and used. Commonly called "Everybody's Medicines", their use did not require the sanction of spiritual dreams or ceremonies. They could be gathered, stored and administered by anyone; many of them would have been found among typical family supplies of the past.

The various medicine uses are described in past tense, out of respect to contemporary medicine people, who may still be using them today.

16

ALUM ROOT *(Heuchera)*
A plant with blue flowers and many roots, whose native name was "Dry Root".

The roots can be boiled into a brew for stomach aches, cramps and diarrhoea. The cooled brew was used as a wash for sore eyes, or as a drink for sore throats. Also given to horses to treat coughing. The horse was thrown down and tied, a tube (such as a plant stem) was stuck into its mouth and the brew poured in until enough was swallowed.

The leaves can be chewed and applied wet to sores and swollen places on the body; also mixed with fat and boiled in water to treat saddle sores on horses.

BEARGRASS *(Yucca glauca)*
Also called Yucca and Soapweed, or by its native name, "Sharp Vine". The roots were boiled in water and used as a hair wash by the people of many tribes. Broken and sprained bones were treated by being held in the steam of the grated roots boiling in water. These gratings were also applied as an antiseptic on cuts and wounds.

BANEBERRY *(Actaea rubra)*
This plant has two species, one with red berries, the other with white; both were known as "Black Roots" in the native language. A potent brew was made from these roots to treat coughs and colds.

BEARDTONGUE *(Pentstamone)*
Because of its flavour, this plant was called "Tastes-like-Fire". A brew of it was used to treat stomach aches and cramps, as well as to stop vomiting.

CUT-LEAVED ANEMONE *(Anemone multifida)*
Because of the woolly tops on its fruiting heads, this plant was called "Looks-like-a-Plume". The woolly material was burned on hot coals and inhaled for headaches.

INDIAN HEMP *(Apocynum cannabinum)*
A plant known as "Little Blanket" or "Many Spears", generally found in dense brush and on high cliffs. The roots were brewed and used as a laxative. The brew was also used as a hair wash. The dried leaves were sometimes smoked.

LARKSPUR *(Delphinium)*
Known as "Blue Leaves", the leaves of this plant were brewed for kidney troubles and also used as an eye wash.

LOCOWEED *(Oxytropis)*
Called "Rattle Sounds" because the ripe seeds inside the pods rattle, especially when the wind blows. The leaves were chewed and the juice swallowed for sore throats and coughing spasms, especially among children. A brew was made from the leaves to treat sores on the head.

MINT *(Mentha arvensis)*
Known as "Strong Smell", mint leaves were brewed into a popular drink, which was especially used for upset stomachs. Sometimes the leaves were chewed and swallowed for chest pains.

PUFF BALLS

Known as "Dusty Stars", they symbolized remnants of fallen Stars from the sky. The puffy substance was used to catch sparks in primitive fire making kits. They were also held against bleeding noses to stop the flow of blood, or used to cover cuts on the bodies of horses. The yellow contents were brewed for a drink in cases of haemorrhage. They were also used as a compress for hemorrhoids and by menstruating women.

PRAIRIE CROCUS *(Anemone patens)*

Called "Early Old Man", because it matures and dries up quickly in the Spring. The small roots of this plant were brewed and given to women to cause speedy childbirth, else an abortion. The crushed leaves were bound to itchy parts of the body.

PRAIRIE SMOKE *(Geum triflorum)*

Called "Lying-on-its-Belly", because the roots grow along close to the ground. These are dug up, scraped and washed, then crushed and boiled to treat sore throats; also sore and swollen eyes. They were a medicine for snowblindness.

The roots were also crushed and mixed with melted grease to treat sore gums, by washing or gargling.

The roots were melted with kidney fat to treat stomach problems, including ulcers; also to treat body sores, including chapped lips, sores and blisters from riding, and sore nipples from nursing.

A brew made from the leaves was given to persons spitting blood.

The ripe seeds were gathered from the white flowers and crushed to make a perfume.

SAGE *(Artemisia gnapholodes)*

This species was called "Man Sage" and used mainly by men. A few leaves of this were added to many other medicine brews for extra strength. A decoction of the leaves was used to treat coughs; the leaves were chewed to stimulate appetite; soft leaves were placed inside nostrils to stop bleeding; several were chewed and used as a poultice, in the nose or on other cuts and sores.

Sage leaves were added to dried meat for seasoning (though removed before the meat was eaten!). Many hunters placed sage leaves in the nose and mouth of whatever animals they killed on the hunt, as an act of purification.

Sage leaves were the most common form of "toilet paper" in primitive times. They also served as deodorants, being placed under the armpits, between the legs and inside of moccasins. They were also placed on fire to create a smudge helpful in driving away mosquitoes and flies.

SAGE *(Artemisia frigida)*

Known as "Women's Sage", this species was used by Blackfeet women for about the same purposes as the previous was used by men. Its most important use was as a menstrual pad. The tops were brewed to treat heartburn and mountain fever. Horses with back sores are often seen rolling in patches of sage to treat themselves.

SNOWBERRY *(Symphoricarpos occidentalis)*

A common shrub with white berries, its native name was "Weasel Eyes". A decoction was made from the yellow roots to stop the heavy blood of menstruating women.

SQUAW ROOT *(Perideridia gairdneri)*

Known as "Double Root", it was a popular food item as well as medicine. A strong brew was made from the root for kidney ailments. The brew was also poured into the nostrils of people and horses to treat catarrh. The chewed root was swallowed for sore throat or used as a poultice on swellings.

SWEET CICELY *(Osmobiza chilensis)*

Known as "Smell Root", it was considered to have unusual powers in connection with esoteric rituals and practices. It was also made into a popular medicine brew for coughs, colds and pneumonia. Mares were forced to chew and swallow the root to prepare them for foaling.

SWEETGRASS *(Hierochloe odorata)*

"Sweet Smell" was not only the most popular Blackfoot incense, it was also added to many medicinal brews and mixtures. Alone, it was chewed and applied to swellings or boiled and used as a hair wash.

VIOLET *(Viola adunca)*

Called "Blue Mouths", the leaves were chewed and used as a poultice, or boiled into a brew for children who had breathing problems.

WESTERN WILD PARSLEY *(Lomatium simplex)*

The roots were a popular food item known as "Big Turnip". It was also chewed and made into a poultice to treat sores in the mouth and ears, to ease earaches and swollen ears, or to relieve bloodshot eyes (over which it was held in place by a heated cloth). A brew of it was given for chest pains.

WHITLOW GRASS *(Draba species)*

Because the stem of this grass rises from a circle of small leaves it was known as "Centre Grass". Its roots were made into a bitter drink to cause abortion.

WILD BERGAMOT *(Mondardo fistulosa)*

Called "Single Young Man", this plant was a common ingredient in many medicine mixtures. The blossoms were brewed alone to make an eyewash, or together with the leaves to make a drink for stomach aches.

YARROW *(Achillea Millefolium)*

Because of its appearance, this plant was called "Having-a-Pine-Stem". The white flowers were chewed to make a poultice for swellings, including mumps. Leaves were brewed into a drink for liver ailments and hemorrhages. A thick brew was given for raw throats. Several cups of the brew were given to speed up labour during childbirth. Horses were treated with the brew if they had sore eyes. The leaves of the plant were also used as incense.

FLATHEAD MEDICINES

OF THE MOUNTAINS AND VALLEYS

Information from Jerome and Agnes Vanderberg

ALUM ROOT *(Heuchera cylindrica)*
The fresh or dried root of this plant was boiled into a tea to stop diarrhoea. For quicker action the root was peeled and chewed. It was the most reliable cure for such conditions. Medically, this plant is valuable as an astringent and as a cure for dysentery.

BEARBERRY *(Arctostaphylos uva-ursi)*
The same leaves used as Kinni kinnick for smoking were also used for medicine by the people. They were powdered and placed over burns to help with healing. For earache the leaves were smoked in a pipe until the stem got hot. The stem was then removed from the bowl and the hot smoke was blown through it into the aching ear. Medically, the plant is valued as an astringent, tonic, and diuretic used in treating ulcerations of the kidneys, bladder, and urinary tract.

BITTERROOT *(Lewisia rediviva)*
The root was boiled into a strong tea to increase the milk flow of nursing mothers. In recent years, the people have learned of another cure from the Cree people. They boil some of the peeled roots and then drink the brew for heart trouble and pleurisy.

BUTTERCUP *(Raunuculus species)*
The whole plant was crushed and applied as a poultice to open sores. A piece of buckskin was placed over the top of it. It is said to form a scab over the sore, which then allows the wound to heal.

CATNIP *(Nepta cataria)*
The people obtained this plant from members of the Cree Tribe, who called it the "twenty minute fever medicine". They made a tea from the stems and leaves and gave it to a person who had a high fever. The tea caused the person to sweat, which brought down the fever in a very short time.

CHOKECHERRY *(Prunus virginiana)*

The dried sap that can be found on chokecherry bushes was melted in warm water, strained and used for eye drops. Some tribes made a tea from the bark to give strength to new mothers.

COTTONWOOD *(Populus trichocarpa)*

Cottonwood leaves were used as a poultice over boils. A whole leaf - green or dry - was fastened over the boil and replaced regularly.

FALSE HELLEBORE *(Veratrum viride)*

The name for this plant was "Sneeze Root", both in the Flathead and Blackfoot languages. The root was dried and powdered. The powder was used like snuff, which caused violent sneezing. This cleared the nasal passages and helped relieve congestion and head colds.

Medically, the plant is valued as a powerful sedative to nervous, respiratory, and circulatory systems, including high blood pressure.

GRAND FIR *(Abies grandis)*

The bark of this tree is covered with small bubbles of pitch. This pitch smells like mentholatum and was used similarly; people rubbed it on the throat and chest for colds. Other tribes put pieces of the pitch in the corners of their eyes at night for soreness. An eyewash was made by boiling the needles in a small amount of water.

GUM PLANT *(GRindelia howellii)*

The Flathead name for this plant is "Indian Horseshoe". It was rubbed on the hooves of horses to give them protection. It was also boiled into a tea as a medicine for tuberculosis and for various other ailments, including asthma and bronchitis.

HONEYSUCKLE *(Lonicera involucrata)*

The berries of this plant were eaten as a powerful laxative - only three or four doing the job. Children were kept away from the bushes whenever the people camped near them.

KITTEN TAILS *(Besseya rubra)*

The roots of this were used, fresh or dry, to make a potent tasting tea for colds.

MEADOW RUE *(Thalictrum occidentale)*

The dried seeds were gathe red and boiled into a tea for colds and chills. Sometimes Sweetgrass was added to the brew to make it more potent.

MOUNTAIN LAUREL *(Ceanothus velutinus)*

Dried and powdered leaves were mixed with fat and put on burns to heal them. Medically, the plant is valued as an astringent - it causes the body tissues to contract and thus close up wounds.

OREGON GRAPE *(Berberis repens)*

The root was made into a powerful tea for various ailments of the reproductive system. It was used to help a new mother deliver her afterbirth. Some women drank the tea regularly as a contraceptive. Gonorrhoea and syphilis were treated with the drink. Medically, the root is said to contain alkaloids which stimulate smooth muscle tissue such as that in the uterus.

PINEAPPLE WEED *(Matricaria matricarioides)*
The leaves of the plant were made into a tea to help deliver the after-birth. Sometimes a green tree lichen (Evernia species) was mixed with the leaves. The tea was also given to young girls for menstrual cramps.
Medically, the plant has mild tonic qualities.

PLANTAIN *(Plantago major)*
Infected sores and tumours were treated with a covering of Plantain leaves, after they were soaked in hot water to soften them. The covering was said to draw out pus.

PUCCON *(Lithospermum ruderale)*
The leaves of this plant were brewed for a remedy in cases of diarrhoea.

PUFFBALL *(Lycoperdon species)*
The brown and powdery spores of puffballs were rubbed on the cheeks and eyelids of babies to put them to sleep.

QUAKING ASPEN *(Populus tremuloids)*
The bark of this tree was boiled and used to reduce ruptures in men and women. Other tribes used the same brew as a remedy for syphilis.

RIBGRASS *(Plantago purshii)*
The plant was used fresh or dried as a packing around aching teeth.

ROCKY MOUNTAIN JUNIPER *(Juniperus scopulorum)*
The branches and needles were boiled to make a tea for colds. Other tribes also used the tea for coughing, ticklish throats and asthma.

SAGE *(Artemisia species)* There are over two hundred species of sage and over sixty of these have medicinal values as tonics, stimulants, anaesthetics and so on.

Wormwood Sage *(dracunculus)* was boiled in water and then used to reduce swollen feet and legs. The brew was used as a bath and rub, after it had cooled down. The plant was also dried andpowdered for use on open sores. Many tribes steamed the plants in their sweat baths to help with rheumatism, stiffness, and aching bones and muscles.

Western Mugwort *(ludoviciana)* was boiled into a bitter brew for colds and pneumonia.

Sagebrush *(tridentata)* was also boiled into a bitter brew for colds and pneumonia.

SNOWBERRY *(Symphoricarpos occidentalis)*
A tea was made from the stems to help deliver the after-birth of a new mother. The mashed berries were applied to the scabs of cuts and burns for better healing. The root was sometimes made into a potent brew for venereal disease.

SORREL *(Rumex occidentalis)*

The roots of this grass were boiled and drank for syphilis and gonorrhoea. Pioneers used to take it internally and locally for sores and boils.

STINGING NETTLE *(Urtica species)*

The leaves were boiled and given as a drink to persons suffering from "fits". The brew was also used as a foot bath for persons with rheumatism and to improve circulation and purify the blood.

SUMAC *(Rhus glabra)*

A tea was made from the green or dried branches of the tree as a cure for tuberculosis. The patient was required to drink several cups full each day, and to refrain from using sugar or salt. The berries were used as a powerful physic - three or four of them were enough to clean out the body.

SWEET CICELY *(Osmorhiza species)*

One species (obtusa) was the main remedy used by the Flathead people for colds and sore throats. The root was either boiled and drunk or else chewed directly. the root was also mashed and placed around a sore tooth.

Another species *(occidentalis)* was made into a pleasant tasting tea for children's colds.

TANSY *(Tanacetum vulgare)*

The leaves were crushed and applied to burns to help with healing. Some people made a tea from the leaves to relieve general ill feeling. Medically, the tea is valued for reducing fever and correcting menstrual disorders. It is mildly poisonous.

VIOLET *(Viola species)*

The roots of wild violets were brewed into a drink given to children for colds. The roots were also boiled and mashed and applied as a poultice for mumps.

VIRGIN'S BOWER *(Clematis hisutissima)*

Itching skin was treated with this plant after it was boiled in a little water. The itchy area was moistened and the boiled plant was rubbed over it very thoroughly.

WATER LILY *(Nuphar species)*

The roots of water lilies were baked in pits, peeled, mashed and applied as poultices to open and infected sores.

WESTERN YELLOW PINE *(Pinus ponderosa)*

The common Ponderosa Pine provided several remedies.
People with muscular pains used to take the pine boughs into the sweat lodge and beat themselves on the painful areas. The pine needles were heated and placed on the mother's abdomen to help deliver the after-birth. Backaches and rheumatism were treated with a salve made by melting the pitch from the tree together with animal fat. The salve was applied to a piece of buckskin with which the affected area was then covered. Other people applied a similar salve to open sores and inflamed eyes.

WILD BERGAMOT *(Monardo fistulosa)*

Next to Sweet Cicely, this plant was the favourite one for curing colds, fevers and coughs. The plant was made into a tea, which was also drunk as a general tonic. The leaves were also packed around sore teeth. Medically, the plant is sometimes used as a substitute for quinine. It has also been found to have antiseptic uses on skin and in nasal passages.

WILD GERANIUM *(Geranium viscosissimum)*

Warts and corns were removed after they were softened by a cream made form this plant. The root was boiled until a cream-like scum formed on top of the water. This cream was applied to a small pad which was kept over the wart or corn for several days. Sometimes the milky sap was squeezed from the fresh stem of the plant and used in the same way.

Nursing mothers with milk fever and painful swollen breasts were treated with applications of the hot, mashed root. A strip of buckskin or cloth was wound around the breast over the paste.

Horses were treated for sores, cuts and rope burns with applications of the same paste.

WILD MINT *(Mentha arvensis)*

Mint tea was a common brew given for colds. The green leaves were also packed around sore teeth. It is said that the leaves burn worse than the toothache.

WILD ROSE *(Rosa woodsii)*

The roots were boiled to make an eyewash. Medically, they have been used for the same purpose.

WILLOW *(Salix species)*

Willow bark was chewed and applied to cuts and sores to reduce pain and help with healing. Medically, willow bark has been found to contain the drug salicin, which is a mild pain reliever.

YARROW *(Achillea millefolium)*

The stem and leaves were made into a bitter tea for colds. The long leaves were also applied to wounds and sores to help heal them. They were either applied directly, or mashed with water and applied as a paste. Other people drank yarrow tea as a general tonic. Medically, the tea has been used as a remedy for coughs and colds, while the leaves are good for healing external wounds and sometimes internal hemorrhages.

MEDICINE PLANTS OF THE CANADIAN PRAIRIES
USED BY THE CREE AND SAULTEAUX PEOPLE

ALDER *(Alnus Crispa)*

Headaches were treated by covering the patient's head with a blanket while inhaling steam from boiling, crushed alder twigs. Speckled Alder (Alnus Incana) was used for treating sores, by boiling the inner bark, then drinking some of the brew were and applying the rest to the sores. Drops of the same brew used to treat sore eyes.

BLUEBERRY *(Vaccinium Canadiase)*

The dried flowers are placed on a hot stone or pan and the smoke inhaled for headache. The inner part of roots were mashed into a poultice to treat rheumatism and lumbago.

BISHOP'S CAP *(Mitella nudo)*

The root was chewed for sore tongue, or boiled and drunk for diarrhoea.

CHERRIES

The inner bark of pin cherries (Prunue Pennsylvanic) was chewed for sore throats and gums. It was also dried and ground, then applied to cuts and wounds to stop bleeding.

CRANBERRY *(Viburnum Paucifloum)*

The root or inner bark was chewed for toothache; also applied as a poultice for burns.

CURRANT *(Ribes Hudsonianum)*

Black currant roots or dried leaves were boiled into a brew for diarrhoea or stomach cramps.

FERN *(Dryopteris Spinvlosa)*

Scrapings of the roots were boiled into a tea for menstrual cramps. The leaves were steeped and applied to swellings.

HONEYSUCKLE *(Lonicara Dicica)*

Scrapings of the roots are boiled, cooled then given as an enema for constipation. A decoction of the inner bark was used to treat snow blindness.

JUNIPER *(Juniperus Communis)*

The needles were mashed, then mixed with warm water to make a poultice for burns.

LABRADOR TEA *(Ledum)*

The dried leaves were powdered and placed in the nose for nose bleed. Crushed leaves were mixed with warm water to make a poultice for boils. A brew of the boiled whole plant was used for heart troubles and chest pains. Burns were treated with a poultice made of Labrador Tea and Wild Ginger, mixed with oil or lard.

LILY *(Numphaea advena)*

Roots of the Yellow Pond Lily were crushed and made into a poultice for swellings, or boiled into a brew applied to skin sores.

MILKWEED *(Aselepies Syriaca*

Twigs were boiled and the brew drunk regularly by mothers whose breast milk would not flow.

MINT *(Mentha Arvonsie)*

The dried leaves were crushed, mixed with water, sprinkled on hot stones (as in a sweatbath) and inhaled for head aches, else placed under a blanket covering the legs for soreness.

MOSS *(Lycoperdales)*

Dried spores were used to treat nose bleed and wounds, places on the navel and umbilic parts of newborn babies.

MOUNTAIN ASH *(Sorbus Americana)*

The inner bark was chewed for toothache and sore throat. The twigs were boiled for a brew to treat indigestion. The inner bark or small branches were boiled for rheumatism, part of the brew was drunk, the rest applied as a poultice to sore areas.

PLANTAIN *(Plantago)*

The green leaf was applied to treat burns.

POPLAR *(Populus Tremulordes)*

The inner bark was made into a brew to treat colds and consumption; drops of the brew were used to treat sore eyes. Young leaves were soaked in cold water overnight and drunk for coughs.

REED GRASS *(Phraguites Communie)*

A handful of the grass was boiled and drunk for constipation.

WILD ROSE *(Rosa Blands)*

Dried buds and flowers were powdered, mixed with fat and used to numb toothache. Roots of Wild Rose and raspberry were boiled together and drunk for fever.

SARSAPARILLA *(Aurila Sudicaulis)*

Toothaches and sore gums treated with a decoction of crushed roots; especially used for teething babies. Drops of the same brew were put into ears for earache, or rubbed on forehead for headache. Labour pains, menstrual cramps and excessive menstrual bleeding were treated with drinks of a brew made by combining sarsaparilla stalks or roots with the whole plant of spiny wood fern *(Dryopteris Spinielosa)*.

SPRUCE *(Picea Mariana and Canadinsis)*

Black spruce needles were chewed and applied as a poultice to burns, cuts and wounds; sometimes the outer bark was chewed and applied instead. A brew made with the crushed cones was drunk for diarrhoea, or for passing blood. A decoction to treat cramps was made by boiling the inner bark of white spruce; also used for excessive menstrual bleeding and for labour pains.

STRAWBERRY *(Frageria)*

The roots of wild strawberries were scraped into a brew used to treat diarrhoea, as well as heart problems.

TAMARACK *(Larix Larcina)*

A decoction of boiled root scrapings was used to treat diarrhoea. The inner bark was boiled and made into a poultice to treat burns, bruises, swellings and wounds.

WILLOW *(Salix Sogra)*

Roots of the swamp willow were crushed and applied to cuts and wounds to stop bleeding. A decoction of the roots was used to treat diarrhoea.

PLANTS USED BY THE THOMPSON INDIANS

OF BRITISH COLUMBIA

ANEMONE *(Anemone multifida)*
Called "Bleeding Nose Plant" by the people, its leaves were used for plugging the nose to stop bleeding. For light bleeding, a fresh plant was held under the nose like smelling salts.

BEARBERRY *(Arctostaphylos uva-ursi)*
This is the popular plant often called Kinnikinnick. The leaves and stems were boiled to make a wash for sore eyes. The brew was also drunk as a diuretic and tonic for the kidneys and bladder.

BLACK HAWTHORN *(Crataegus douglassi)*
A brew was made from the sap, stems, bark and sometimes the roots and used as a stomach medicine. The spines were used to probe boils and ulcers.

DEVIL'S CLUB *(Echinopanax horridum)*
A drink was made for indiges tion and for stomach problems by crushing the fresh stems and soaking them in water. The same drink was also used as a general tonic and blood purifier. Sometimes it was boiled first, although it then became a laxative, as well. An ointment for swellings was made by burning the stems and mixing ashes with grease.

FALSE SOLOMON'S SEAL *(Vagnera racemosa)*
A brew made with the berries of this plant was used as a medicine for stomach problems and by menstruating women. The plant may be mistaken for that of Baneberries, which are poisonous.

HONEYSUCKLE *(Lonicera involucrata)*
The leaves were boiled and washed and then placed on swollen parts of the body. To make this medicine stronger the leaves were first bruised. The berries can be eaten, although they are not very tasty. The people called this the "Grizzly Bear Plant", because of that animal's fondness for the berries.

27

LODGEPOLE PINE *(Pinus contorta)*

The people collected the gum from this tree's cones and bark. They boiled it and mixed it with melted deer's fat to make an ointment for rheumatism, as well as general soreness of muscles and joints. The same ointment was rubbed on the throat, sides of the neck, and chest or back to relieve congestion, coughs and sore throats. The ointment was especially effective when it was vigorously rubbed on after a steam bath or while the patient sat in front of a hot fire.

NETTLE *(Urtica lyalli)*

The plant was teased up, dipped in water, and then rubbed on parts of the body that were affected by stiffness and soreness of the joints and muscles.

PIPISISSEWA *(Chimaphila umbellata occidentalis)*

A plant of known tonic qualities, this one was called "Childbirth's Medicine" by the Knife People. Leaves from the plant, fresh or dried, were chewed before and during the time of childbirth. A little of the plant was swallowed now and then, to make the experience more bearable.

QUAKING ASPEN *(Populus tremuloides)*

The Knife People made a medicine form this tree for cases of syphilis. They gathered stems and small branches form the very young trees and boiled them slowly for a couple of days. The patient had to sit in the cooled brew for several hours at a time and wash himself with it. He also had to drink several cupfuls of the brew every day. The bathing was done daily for two to four days, or until he was relieved of aching bones and swellings. The brew had to be given longer than the baths.

SAGE *(Artemisia tridentata)*

A brew made by boiling the leaves and stems was drunk for colds, consumption and emaciation. Often a pad was made from the leaves and tied to the nostrils, or some of the leaves were used to plug the nostrils up.

SERVICEBERRY *(Amelanchier alnifolia)*

The stems and twigs were boiled and given to women as a drink after childbirth. Often the new mother was also bathed in the brew. A strong brew made with the bark was given as a drink to help expel the afterbirth. The same brew was also used generally as a tonic.

SPURGE *(Euphorbia glyptosperma)*

The people called this plant "Medicine for Rattlesnake". They rubbed the fresh plant over snake bites, especially those caused by rattlesnakes. It is a poisonous plant that can irritate the skin after prolonged contact.

VALERIAN *(Valeriana sitchenis and sylvatica)*

This plant is noted for its medicinal properties. The people boiled the roots and drank the brew for pains and as a remedy for colds. Cuts and wounds were treated with this plant - as a poultice made by pounding the roots or the whole plant, or by chewing the fresh leaves until well mixed with saliva, or by washing the fresh stems and leaves and applying

them directly. Out of season the dried roots were crushed into a fine powder and sprinkled on the wounds. Men in the Old Days always kept some of this plant in their Medicine Bags in case of sudden need.

YARROW *(Achillea millefolium)*

Called "Chipmunk's Tail" by the Knife People, because of the appearance of the leaves of the plant. The whole plant was boiled as a general tonic. The plant was also used as a wash for sore eyes, for chapped or cracked hands, for pimples, skin rashes, and for insect and snake bites. A wash was made by bruising the plant or crushing it into a pulp, and mixing that with cold water. Plants used for making things

CATTAIL *(Typha latifolia)*

The stalks of the Common Cattail were used for bedding. The stems and leaves were stripped and made into bags and mats. The fluffy heads were gathered and used as a substitute for down in stuffing pillows and making beds.

DOGBANE *(Apocynum cannabinum)*

This plant is known as Indian Hemp. The inner bark was gathered in the fall and treated. It made a soft but very strong cord, from which was made rope, nets, snares, clothing and thread. Sometimes it was used for bowstrings, in place of sinew.

JUNIPER *(Juniperus scopulorum)*

The wood was used for making bows, drums, and clubs, as well as for hafting implements.

REED GRASS *(Phargmites communis)*

The stems of this plant were one of the most commonly used materials for baskets made by the Knife People.

SAGE *(Artemesia frigida)*

Sagebrush was commonly used by the Knife People in the smouldering fires with which they smoked their tanned skins. Twined Sagebrush twigs were used to make various kinds of containers, such a squivers. The bark was peeled from the stem and used to weave saddle blankets.

SERVICEBERRY *(Amelancier alnifolia)*

The hard wood was very popular for making handles and tools, such as root diggers.

SILVER FIR *(Abies grandis)*

The bark from this tree was used for covering lodges and making canoes. The people called this fir "Sweet Branch", because of its fragrant leaves. The smaller branches were thus often used for bedding, and sometimes for lodge flooring.

WILD GINGER *(Asarum caudatum)*

The whole plant was used as bedding for infants.

DESERT PLANTS OF THE HOPI PEOPLE

INDIAN RICE GRASS *(Oryzopsis hymenoides)*
A tall grass which is common all over North America. When the grass is ripe the seeds fall to the ground in abundance. The Hopi gathered these seeds - especially in times of famine. They are said to be very palatable when cooked or ground up into meal.

DROPSEED *(Sporobolus species)*
Several varieties and sizes of this grass produce seeds that were gathered after they ripened and fell free from the chaff.

WILD POTATO *(Solanum jamesii)*
This plant belongs to the same family as the Deadly Nightshade, some of whose members are very poisonous. The Wild Potato grows like a weed in the Hopi country. Its roots are like small potatoes, the size of cherries. They were boiled in water and mixed with a salty type of clay - called potato clay - to neutralize their bitter taste.

CACTUS
The Hopi used several species of cactus for food. Most of these were obtained by trade from other tribes whose countries offered better selections. Some species similar to the Prickly Pear were gathered. The joints were boiled and stripped of their thorns. The boiled joints were then dipped into a juice made form boiling baked sweet corn.

The fruits of the Cholla Cactus were boiled and eaten with Squash. The roots of this cactus were a popular medicine for curing diarrhoea.

WILD BEANS *(Phaseolus acutifolis latifolis)*
Also known as Teparies, several species of these small, wild beans grow in the Hopi country. They are an ancient Hopi food. They were parched before being cooked.

SUMAC *(Rhus trilobata)*
The Hopi People made a refreshing drink from Sumac Berries. The plant was used in several other ways. The berries served in wool dying preparation. The twigs were used to make baskets and baby cradles; also as a ceremonial fuel in kivas. The buds were used as a perfume.

SPIDERFLOWER *(Cleome serrulata)*
Also known as "Rocky Mountain Beeweed", this plant is common in many areas of the continent. The Hopi gathered great quantities of the young plants and boiled them as vegetables.

AMARANTH FAMILY
One weed in this family is known in Latin as Acanthon wrightii. It is celebrated as an ancient Hopi food which has often saved the people during famines. It is cooked as a vegetable, especially with meat. It was gathered and strung in long bunches to dry. Another member of this family is known as Amaranthus blitoides (Pigweed). It is common all over the continent. It was gathered and cooked as a vegetable and its seeds were crushed into a meal.

GOOSEFOOT FAMILY
Several members of this family were cooked as foods by the old time Hopi, including Lamb's Quarters and a species known as Saltbush, or Atriplex in Latin.

MESCAL *(Agave)*
This plant was obtained by the Hopi from the Havasupai People, who prepared it by baking the young buds and leaves in large earth ovens. The baked preparation was made into a drink by the Hopi, after it was soaked in water.

MARIPOSA LILY *(Calonchortus aureus)*
The roots of this plant were eaten raw by the Hopi. They also made their "Sacred Yellow Pollen", for use in ceremonies, by grinding together the seeds and flowers of this plant.

CATTAIL *(Typha angustifolia)*
Cattail stems are given as presents to Hopi children during the Kachina dances. They are chewed like sugar cane. The mature heads of the plants were often mixed with tallow and chewed like gum.

JUNIPER *(Juniperus utahensis)*
Juniper has long been a major source of wood for the people of the treeless deserts. The bark is used as tinder for fire making, the sticks as firewood. Straight pieces of the wood were even used for construction. The tart berries were prepared in several ways so that they could be eaten. They were also used inside of rattles and as beads on necklaces.

The Hopi used Juniper as a special medicine for women. The leaves were boiled into a tea and given to a woman right after childbirth. While the new mother was recovering, she was given the juice from brewed Juniper leaves with or in every meal, to help clean her out. Her clothes and body were washed several times with a mixture of the same brew. It was respected as a powerful cleansing agent for the body and mind.

PINYON *(Pinus edulis)*
No food list of the Southwest deserts would be complete without mentioning the popular Pinyon nuts, which have been an important staple for the desert people throughout time. The nuts are prepared in a variety of ways - roasted, boiled and crushed.

FOOD OF THE ANCIENTS

As told by Medicine Flower

(Excerpt from: Cushing, Frank Hamilton **ZUNI BREADSTUFF**)

"First among (wild seeds) was a kind of purslane or portulaca, not unlike the garden pests of the same genus in the East. This plant bore plentifully a small black, very starchy and white-kernelled seed. It was gathered by pulling the plants just before the seed had ripened, then drying and threshing them either by agitation or by pounding them over mats or screens. A method of gathering such seeds as had advanced too far toward maturity was to sweep up the surface, usually sandy, of the ground on which they grew, dust and all, and afterward to carefully winnow the seeds from the soil."

"Various nuts and seeds were quite similarly prepared for food, and several varieties of them were not infrequently compounded to form a single kind of bread or cake."

"The possible rival of (soapweed) was made from the hearts of the mescal plant or the mature agave. When large quantities of these cabbage-like hearts had been gathered, great pits were dug in gravelly knolls. Within and around the pits, fires were built, which were kept burning whole days or nights. When the ground had been thoroughly heated, the mescal hearts were thrown in on a layer of coarse leaves of the same plant, with which they were also covered. They were then buried deep in the hot gravel. Huge fires were kept burning over the mounds thus formed until the mescals were considered done."

"Meanwhile crowds gathered, dances of a semi-sacred, though not very refined nature, were celebrated, and the pits wee opened amid universal rejoicing. The time was divided between riotous feasting and serious mastication of the baked, already very sweet leaves, to separate them from the fiber. The pulp or paste thus formed was spread out thinly over large mats, and when dried could be conveniently rolled up for transportation."

"Another and more wholesome method was pursued, if the quantity furnished by the pit proved too much for the maxillary powers of the party. This was to pound the leaves, and, if necessary, moisten them slightly to give them a pulpy consistency, and thus spread and dry them on the plaited mats."

"Although much less valued by the Indians, this kind of food was toothsome and more nutritious, perhaps, than any other preparation."

"Among the sandy defiles of the upper plains, mesas, and mountains, grow abundant low bushes bearing very juicy little yellow berries called 'juice-filled fruitage'. These berries were in high favour with the ancient Zunis as food. They were collected in great quantities and boiled or stewed, forming a sweet but acrid sauce which although not quite so acid, resembled otherwise the cranberry."

"Seeds of the Ancient were sown only by the Beloved, and his herds herded by the Gods of Prey themselves"; (according to Zuni legend) which, interpreted, signifies that he gathered the seed cultivated by the winds and rains alone, and that his herds, the deer, antelope, and other animals of the chase, were so wild that none could watch and follow them save the brotherhood of the coyote and the mountain lion."

"Yet by no means meager were the repasts or limited the cuisine here derived from these apparently precarious sources...."

"Among the high mountains grew many trees which, stripped of their outer bark and scraped, yielded a sappy pulp and sweet fiber - hard of digestion, it is true, but none the less grateful to his meat-sated appetite. Most valued for this kind of food and easy of access with his rude instruments was the yellow pine, thousands of the trunks of which were annually whitened on the southern sides by the scrapers of the ancient Zunis. Oftentimes only the pulp thus obtained was eaten raw, and the stringy, stringent fiber was wrapped into bundles - huge skeins - and carried home for cooking. Some of it was boiled with bony joints of dried meat...."

"Deep down in the sand which bordered, and for a time almost choked, the starved streams issuing from the mountains, were dug the juicy roots of certain rushes which, sweet and earthy in taste, although scarcely more nutritious than the bark-pulp, were like the latter grateful for the variety they afforded. They were eaten raw, or else slightly roasted in the ashes, dipped in salted water, and used as relishes for roasts of jerked meat."

33

"Another root which every child sought and grubbed for with avidity was the.... 'sweet-root', a kind of wild licorice which, nevertheless, differed so far from the product with which we are acquainted that an unwhole some amount of bitter was mingled with its sweet. Doubtless the ancient Zuni, like the modern, dried the root to serve as an ingredient for other foods."

With the advance of the season the rush stems grew tough, the licorice more bitter than ever, and they were replaced with great quantities of watercress, like in taste and appearance, though smaller, the celery we all prize. It grew abundantly in every spring and living streamlet, was boiled and eaten with other food, the residue each day being made into flat, compact cakes, and dried with salt into greenish-black, very stemmy, and indurate bricks, which were packed away for second cookings.

"Another far more nutritious food, but one requiring masterly care in its preparation, was a diminutive wild potato which grew in all bottom-lands favored to any extent with moisture. These potatoes were poisonous in the raw state or whole, but were rendered harmless by the removal of the skin. As they were never larger than nutmegs, this had to be accomplished by a preliminary boiling with ashes. Afterward the potatoes were again stewed and eaten with the water they had been boiled in, usually with the addition of wild onions as a relish.

"A very important addition, too, were these onions, which grew in springtime under many of the ranges of cliffs throughout the Southwest, and although true onions, resemble in size and appearance the Eastern garlic. They were invariably eaten raw, in which condition they were almost strong enough to temporarily benumb the organs of taste, flood the eyes, and annihilate all sense of everything in the region of smell save themselves. Their Zuni name (is) 'stinking root-nuts'."

"Apace with the season more and more plants furnished food material. Everywhere that rain had fallen on the lower plains grew in fitful and brief luxuriance a small variety of milkweed which bore in abundance little seed-vesicles resembling those of the common mustard.... called 'hanging pods'. Divested of their skins, they were eaten raw, or boiled with other foods, or, again, toasted in hot ashes and soaked in the all-important brine-sauce with mashed onions."

"A kind of wild, hard-shelled squash, from which doubtless were derived varieties of the true garden plant cultivated by the Zunis today, grew abundantly in moist arroyos, the fruit of which, while still green, was cooked in various ways. Principally, it was boiled to paste, mixed liberally with rancid suet, and fried on hot stone slabs. As such it resembled eggplant fried in butter...."

"A great luxury was a kind of puff-ball, or fungus, produced in warm seasons in spontaneous liberality by the rains. These were peeled, toasted, and eaten with a sauce of brine and ground onions, flavoured with the aromatic seeds of certain caraway plants native to the country."

"During early summer the unripe seedy pods of the yucca, a quart or two of which may sometimes be gathered from a single stalk or spike, were much sought after by the ancient Zunis. They were boiled excessively either in water or in water and ashes. When afterward cleansed they had much the appearance of gherkins, which indeed they prove similar to in taste when pickled in vinegar. They were eaten either plain or with a liberal allowance of the flavoured brine-sauce."

"First to ripen, first, too, in importance among the fruits, was the datila (soapweed).... Few who have not visited the Southwest in autumn imagine that, dry and sterile though it be throughout most of the year, a fruit rivalling in its size, shape, color and exceeding sweetness the banana, grows there in abundance on the warmer plains. Yellow and red, this long, pulpy fruit hangs in clusters so heavy that they bend or sometimes break the stalks that bear them."

"Yet, however delicious, these....may not be eaten raw in large quantity with impunity.... After great stores of the fruit had been gathered in little, square burden-baskets by the men and heaped in shady, cool places, it was peeled by the women and thoroughly masticated. By this means not only were the seeds separated from the pulp, but the latter was thus made ready to be set away in water-tight basket-bowls for fermentation. By fermentation an agreeable pungent taste was added and the saliva acting on the glutinous or mucilaginous ingredients heightened the sweetness. The process was stopped by excessive boiling, which reduced the pulp to homogeneous paste, which on cooling was kneaded into little, flat cakes. The latter, when partially dried were pounded together and rolled into large cylinders. In the course of time, these cylinders grow quite solid and gummy, and semi-translucent like the gelatin ink rollers used by printers. In taste the food resembles black licorice. A little slice being hacked off was immersed in two or three quarts of water. When thoroughly soaked, it was stirred, churned, squeezed, and strained, until a dark-red, pasty fluid was formed; hardly any delicacy known to the ancient Zunis ranked more highly or commanded such extravagant bargains in barter with the surrounding tribes."

"Another favourite berry was the small and equally acrid fruit of the wild currant, called in Zuni.... 'first to leaf out', which grew along the edges of malpais mesas in verdant luxuriance rare to be seen in the Southwest."

"Like the two latter, the chokecherry, or 'bitter hanging fruit', formed the ingredient of frequent sauces."

"The wild plum was used not only in the raw and stewed state, but was also dried and preserved for after use."

"A much more abundant fruit, very sweet and aromatic in flavour, was the cedar-berries. They were collected in large quantities, boiled, roasted, or dried and ground to form the meal with which were made several varieties of cake."

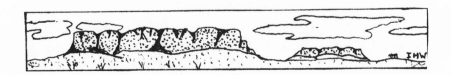

NATIVE WAYS OF GROWING CROPS

In common with native farmers all over the world, prayers were important to American Indians who planted crops far back in ancient times, as they still are to many today. Not only prayers, but ceremonies and rituals accompanied Indian gardening. In fact, the growing of crops was often only the highlight of year-long fertility rites that gave respect to the Earth, as Mother, the Sun, as Father, and to a Creator for making it all.

While some native tribes lived almost exclusively on the meat their hunters obtained, others got most of their food from wild plants and from those they cultivated. That crop growing is an ancient art in North America was proven by remains of corn found in caves of Northern Mexico that were more than six thousand years old! When Columbus arrived on the shores of America he found corn fields eighteen miles long! The seeds he took back to Europe introduced corn to that continent. Today, corn is the third major world crop, after rice and potatoes.

Remains of ancient gardens, found in many parts of North America, usually show signs of the four main native crops: corn, beans squashes, and pumpkins, in that order of importance. Not much variety, until you add wild fish and meat, plus berries and roots of many kinds; garden crops often provided only the staple.

Native corn has six subspecies, which grow in different climates and have various uses. Flint, flour and dent corn were the most important of these, while sweet, pop and pod corn were less commonly grown.

Flint corn is considered the most ancient of all. Its kernels are made up mostly of tough skin, making it a hardy corn which grows best in cold, moist climates, such as the lower regions of Canada, the New England area, and cooler mountain regions of the South.

Flour corn is grown mainly in the hot, dry desert areas of the Southwest. It has no tough skin, being made up mostly of soft starch. For that reason, it is easily ground into flour and meal, the basic food item of Pueblo-dwelling people.

Dent corn is a combination of the other two kinds, having a tough skin which protects its soft starchy interior from rains and other harsh weather in the Southeast, where it has been mainly grown.

While corn is the most important crop Europeans obtained from Ameri can Indians, others include beans, squashes, pumpkins, two varieties of sweet potatoes, tobacco, gourds and the sunflower.

Modern farmers can only marvel when they look at the primitive tools used by natives, such as hoes made by attaching animal shoulder blades to hardwood sticks, or rakes made from a set of deer horns. Yet, the ancient inhabitants of the Salado Valley are said to have worked some 250,000 acres of land, using elaborate systems of canals and wooden locks for irrigation.

While contributing valuable crops to Europeans when they first came to America, Indian farmers were also willing to accept new kinds of crops in exchange. The Hopi provide a good example of these changes. Spaniards were the first Europeans to arrive in their country, during the 1600's, when missionaries came "to save their souls".

The religious efforts ended in failure, when the proud and satisfied Hopi drove the Spaniards out, but not before they had learned to grow wheat, onions, watermelons, peaches and chili peppers. The latter has since become such an important crop that no Pueblo home is complete without a thick bunch of dried red chilies hanging by a doorway.

In the 1870's Mormon missionaries tried where the Spaniards had failed, though with little more success. When they gave up, after some twenty-five years of trying, they left behind improved irrigation systems, plus seeds for growing better squash, as well as sorghum and safflower.

By the early 1900's , Hopi farmers were obtaining all sorts of new seeds from teachers, traders, missionaries, and even anthropologists who came among them. Then, in 1915, a number of Hopi were brought to a large agricultural gathering at the San Diego Exposition, where they met many farmers, including some form other tribes, with much seed exchanging taking place. They came home to instruct their people in such new arts as ordering seeds and plants from the catalogues of far away mail-order places. Throughout all these changes, Hopi farmers have maintained faith in ancient rituals for growing crops and maintaining a natural balance in life.

SOME WORDS ON AGRICULTURE AMONG

THE HIDATSA PEOPLE

by Buffalobird-Woman

This that I am going to tell you of the planting and harvesting of our crops is out of my own experience, seen with my own eyes. In olden times, I know, my tribe used digging sticks and bone hoes for garden tools...

SUNFLOWERS

The first seed that we planted in the spring was Sunflower seed. Ice breaks on the Missouri about the first week in April; and we planted as soon after as the soil could be worked. Our native name for the lunar s0month that corresponds most nearly to April is... Sunflower-planting-Moon.

Planting was done by hoe, or the woman scooped up the soil with her hands. Three seeds were planted in a hill, at the depth of the second joint of a woman's finger.... The hill was heaped up and patted firm with the palm in the same way as we did for Corn.... The hills were placed eight or nine paces apart.... Sometimes all three seeds sprouted and came up together; sometimes only two sprouts; sometimes only one.

Although our Sunflower seed was the first crop to be planted in the Spring, it was the last to be harvested in the Fall.... Our Sunflowers were ready for harvesting when the little petals that covered the seeds fell off, exposing the ripe seeds beneath....

My basket filled, I returned to the lodge, climbed the ladder to the roof, and spread the Sunflower heads upon the flat part of the roof around the smoke hole, to dry. The heads were laid face downward, with the back to the Sun.... When the heads had dried about four days, the seeds were threshed out; and I would fetch in from the garden another supply of heads to dry and thresh.

Sunflower harvest came after we had threshed our Corn; and corn threshing was in the first part of October....frosting of the seeds had an effect upon them that we rather esteemed. We made a kind of oily mortar; but meal made from seed that had been frosted, seemed more oily than that from seed gathered before frost fell....

CORN

Corn planting began the second month after Sunflower-seed was pla nted, that is in May; and it lasted about a month.... We knew when Corn s0planting time came by observing the leaves of the wild Gooseberry bushes.... Old women of the village were going to the woods daily to gather fire wood; and when they saw that the wild Gooseberry bushes were almost in full leaf, they said, "It is time for you to begin planting Corn!"

Excerpt from: Wilson, Gilbert Livingstone
AGRICULTURE OF THE HIDATSA INDIANS

Corn was planted each year in the same hills.... I planted about six to eight grains in a hill. Then with my hands I raked the Earth over the planted grains until the seed lay about the length of my fingers under the soil. Finally I patted the hill firm with my palms.

The Corn hills I planted well apart, because later, in hilling up, I would need room to draw Earth from all directions over the roots to protect them from the Sun, that they might not dry out. Corn planted in hills too close together would have small ears and fewer of them; and the stalks of the plants would be weak, and often dried out.

We Hidatsa women were early risers in the plating season; it was my habit to be up before Sunrise, while the air was cool, for we thought this the best time for garden work.

Having arrived at the field, I would begin one hill, preparing it, as I have said, with my hoe; and so for ten rows each.... about thirty yards; the rows were about four feet apart, and the hills stood about the same distance apart in the row.

The hills all prepared, I went back and planted them, patting down each with my palms, as described. Planting Corn thus by hand was slow work, but by ten o'clock the morning's work was done, as I was tired and ready to go home for my breakfast and rest; we did not eat before going into the field. The ten rows making the morning's planting contained about two hundred and twenty-five hills.

The very last Corn that we planted we sometimes put into a little tepid water, if the season was late. Seed used for replanting hills that had been destroyed by Crows or Magpies we also soaked. We left the seed in the water only a short time, when the water was poured off.

Seed corn thus soaked would have sprouts a third of an inch long four or five days after planting if the weather was warm. This soaked seed produced strong plants, but the first-planted, dry seeds still produced the first ripened ears.

It was usual for the women of a household to do their own planting; but if a woman was sick, or for some reason was unable to attend to her planting, she sometimes cooked a feast, to which she invited the members of her age society and asked them to plant her field for her.

The members of her society would come upon an appointed day and plant her field in a short time; sometimes a half day was enough.

When our Corn was in, we began planting Beans and Squashes. Beans we commonly planted between Corn rows, sometimes over the whole field, more often over a part of it.

SQUASH

Squash seed was planted early in June.... In preparation for planting, we first sprouted the seed.

Usually two or three women did the family planting, working together. One woman went ahead and with her hoe loosened up the ground for a space of about fifteen inches in diameter, for the hill. Care was taken that each hill was made in the place where there had been a hill the year before.... using the same hill thus, each year, made the soil here soft and loose, so that the plants thrived.

One woman.... made a new hill, about fifteen inches in diameter at the base. Following her came another woman who planted the sprouted seeds.

Four seeds were planted in each hill, in two pairs. The pairs should be about twelve inches apart, and the two seeds in each pair, a half inch apart. The seeds were planted rather under, or on one side of the hill, and about two inches deep in the soil.

We had a reason for planting the Squash seeds in the side of the hill. The squash sprouts were soft, tender. If we planted them in level ground the rains would beat down the soil, and it would pack hard and get somewhat crusted, so that the sprouts could not break through; but if we planted the sprouts on the side of the hill, the water from the rains would flow over them and keep the soil soft.

Squashes grow fast, and unless we picked them every four days, we did not think them so good for food. Moreover, Squashes that were four days old we could slice for drying, knowing that the slices would be firm enough to retain their shape unbroken.

We could tell when a Squash was four days old. Its diameter then was about three and a quarter inches.... but we chiefly judged by the colour of the fruit.

We picked a good many Squashes in a season. One year my mother fetched in seventy baskets from our field.

The Squash was sliced from side to side.... less valuable slices had each a hollow in the center, caused by the seed cavity. The better slices.... were spitted on Willow rods to dry. A spit was sharpened at one end to a point. At the other end there was left about an inch of the natural bark like a button, to keep the Squash slices from falling off. The spitted slices were.... then separated about a half inch apart.... One Willow spit held the slices of four Squashes....

Drying rods.... were laid across the upper rails of the stage; and each spit as it was loaded was laid with either end resting on a drying rod.... If the drying Squash got wet after the first day, the slices swelled up and the fruit spoiled.

On the evening of the third day the slices were dry enough to string.

The strings, three to six in number, had been prepared from dry grass. Each string was seven Indian fathoms long; we Hidatsas measure a fathom as the distance between a woman's two outstretched hands. Each grass string had a wooden needle about ten inches long, bound to one end.

All the slices on one spit were now slid off and the worker by a single thrust skewered the wooden needle through them and slid them down to the farther end....

.... The Squash strings were taken out and hung on a fair day; in the morning on the East side; in the afternoon, on the west side of the stage.

On wet days, the Squash strings were left inside the lodge; and if the rain was falling heavily, a tent skin, or scraped rawhides, dried and ready to tan, were thrown over them to protect from dampness. The air in the lodge was damp on a rainy day; and sometimes the roof leaked.

When the strings of Squash were thought to be thoroughly dried, they were ready for storing. A portion was packed in parfleche bags, to be taken to the Winter lodge, or to be used for food on journeys. The rest was stored away in a cache pit, covered with loose Corn.

PLANTING BEANS

Bean planting followed immediately after Squash planting.

Beans were planted in hills the size and shape of Squash hills, or about seven by fourteen inches.... Squash hills, like Corn hills, stood about four feet apart in the row, measuring from center to center; but Bean hills might be placed two feet or less in the row.

Beans.... were very commonly planted.... between our rows of Corn....

I took Beans, three in each hand, held in thumb and first two fingers, and buried them in a side of the hill, two inches deep, by simultaneous thrust of each hand, as I stooped over; the two groups of seeds were six inches apart.

HOEING

We hoed but once, not very many weeds coming up to bother us afterwards. In my girlhood, we were not troubled with mustard and thistles; these weeds have come in with white men.

We did not hoe the Corn alone, but went right through the garden.... Weeds were let lie on the ground, as they were now young and harmless.

I cultivated each hill carefully with my hoe as I came to it; and if the plants were small, I would comb the soil of the hill lightly with my fingers, loosening the earth and tearing out young weeds.

A second hoeing began, it is true, when the Corn silk appeared, but was accompanied by hilling, so that we looked upon it rather as a hilling time. Hilling was done to firm the plants against the wind and cover the roots of the Corn.

Not a great many weeds were found in the garden at hilling time, unless the season had been wet; but weeds at this season are apt to have seeds, so that it was my habit to bear such weeds off the field, that the seeds might not fall and sprout the next season.

With the Corn, the Squashes and Beans were also hilled; but this was an easier task. The Bean hills, especially were made small at first, and hilling them up afterwards was not hard work. If beans were hilled too high the vines got beaten down into the mud by the rains and rotted.

THRESHING

Threshing was in the Fall, after the Beans had ripened and the pods were dead and dried.... When the vines were dry I took out into the field half of an old tent cover and laid it on the ground in an open space made by clearing away the Corn stalks. This tent cover, so laid, was to be my threshing floor.... I took up some of the dry vines and laid them on the tent cover in a heap, about three feet high. I got upon this heap with my moccasined feet and smartly trampled it, now and then standing on one foot, while I shuffled and scraped the other over the dry vines; this was done to shake the Beans loose from their pods.

After the Beans were winnowed, they were dried one more day, either on a tent cover in the garden, or at home on a skin placed on the ground near the drying stage.

Our Bean harvests varied a good deal from year to year; in my father's family, from as little as half a sack, to as much as three barrels.

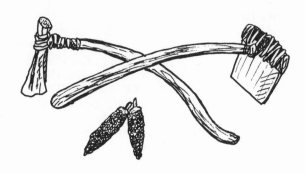

SELECTING SEEDS

In the Spring, when I came to plant Beans, I was very careful to select seed for the following points: seed should be fully ripe; seed should be of full colour; seed should be plump, and of good size.... We were always taught to select seed thus, in my tribe.

Seed Squashes were chosen at the first or second picking of the season. At these pickings, as we went from hill to hill plucking the four-days-old Squashes, we observed what ones appeared the plumpest and finest; and these we left on the vine to be saved for seed. We never chose more than one Squash in a single hill....

There was a good deal of variety in our Squashes. Some were round, some rather elongated.... some dark.... some spotted.... We did not recognize these as different strains, as we did the varieties of Corn; and when I selected Squashes for seed, I did not choose for colour, but for size and general appearance. Squashes of different colour grew in the same hill; and all varieties tasted exactly alike.

.... It was our custom to pluck our Corn until the first frost fell; then to gather our seed Squashes; and afterwards our seed Corn. Some years the first frost fell very early, before we had plucked our first corn; in such seasons we gathered our seed Squashes first, for we never let them lie in the field after the first frost had set in.

I grew our native Squashes in my son Goodbird's garden until four years ago. I stopped cultivating them because my son's family did not seem to care to eat them. Last year a Squash vine came up wild in my son's garden. The Squashes that grew on it were of two colours....

.... For braiding Corn we chose the longest and finest ears. In my father's family we used to braid about one hundred strings.... fifty-four or fifty-five ears were commonly braided to a string.... this number of ears was about the weight that a woman would well carry and put upon the drying stage.... Of these braided strings we selected the very best in the Spring for seed....

When I selected seed Corn, I used only good, full, plump ears....

When I came to plant the Corn, I used only the kernels in the center of the cob for seed, rejecting both the small and the large grains of the two ends....

Corn kept for seed would be best to plant the next Spring; and it would be fertile, and good to plant, the second Spring after harvesting. The third year the seed was not so good; and it did not come up very well. The fourth year the seed would be dead and useless.

Even today, families on this reservation come to me to buy seed Corn and seed Beans. A handful of Beans, enough for one planting, I sell for one calico - enough calico, that is, to make an Indian woman a dress, or about ten yards.

CACHE PITS

We stored our Corn, Beans, Sunflower seed and dried Squash in cache pits for the Winter, much as white people keep vegetables in their cellars.

A cache pit was shaped somewhat like a jug, with a narrow neck at the top. The width of the mouth, or entrance, was commonly about two feet....

Descent into one of these big cache pits was made with a ladder.... In one of these smaller pits, when standing on the floor within, my eyes just cleared the level of the ground above, so that I could look around. When such a pit was half full of Corn, I could descend and come out again, without the help of a ladder.

It took me two days and the good part of a third to dig a cache pit, my mother helping me to carry off the dirt....

When the cache pit was all dug, it had next to be lined with grass. The grass we used for this purpose.... grows about three feet high. It was the long bluish kind that grows near springs and water courses.... other kinds of grass would mould.... Just before using, we took the bundles up on the roof of the Earth lodge, broke the binding ropes and spread the grass out to dry, for one day.

.... A floor was laid on the bottom.... by gathering dead and dry Willow sticks, and laying them evenly and snugly over the bottom of the pit.

Over this Willow floor, the grass, now thoroughly dried was spread evenly, to a depth of about four inches. Grass was then spread over the walls to a depth of three or four inches, and stayed in place with about eight Willow sticks. These were placed vertically against the walls and nailed in place with wooden pins made from the fork of a dead willow....

If the cache pit was a small one, we covered the bottom with a circular piece of skin.... but if the cache pit was a large one, we fitted into the bottom of the skin cover a bull boat, with the Willow frame removed.

We had four cache pits to store grain for my father's family; one held Squash, vegetables, Corn, etc.

A second held shelled yellow Corn. In this cache the usual strings of Corn laid around to protect the shelled grain from the wall, were of white Corn. We did not braid hard yellow Corn. It was Corn that we did not often use for parching.

A third cache held white shelled Corn, protected by the usual braided strings of white Corn.

A fourth cache pit was a small one inside the lodge; here we stored dried wild Turnips, dried Chokecherries, and dried June berries; and any valuables that we could not take with us to our Winter village.

Our cache pits were for the most part located outside the lodge, because Mice were found inside the lodge, and they were apt to be troublesome.

In the cache pit where we stored our yellow Corn, we stored the grain loose, not in sacks.

The Sioux sometimes came up against us in Winter and raided our cached Corn. One Winter (about 1877) they came up and burned our lodges and stole all that was in our cache pits.

MANURE

We Hidatsas did not like to have the dung of Animals in our fields. The Horses we turned into our gardens in the Fall dropped dung; and where they did so, we found little worms and insects. We also noted that where dung fell, many kinds of weeds grew up the next year.

We did not like this, and we therefore carefully cleaned off the dried dung, picking it up by hand and throwing it ten feet or more beyond the edge of the garden plot. We did likewise with the droppings of white men's cattle, after they were brought to us.

Our Corn and vegetables can not grow on land that has many weeds. Now that white men have come and put manure on their fields, these strange weeds brought by them have become common. In old times we Hidatsas kept our gardens clean of weeds.

The government has changed our old way of cultivating Corn and our other vegetables.... our old agriculture has.... fallen into disuse.

At first we Hidatsas did not like Potatoes, because they smelled so strongly! Then we sometimes dug up our Potatoes and took them into our Earth Lodges; and when cold weather came, the Potatoes were frozen, and spoiled. For these reasons, we did not take much interest in our Potatoes, and often left them in the ground, not bothering to dig them.

Other seeds were issued to us, of Watermelons, big Squashes, Onions, Turnips, and other vegetables. Some of these we tried to eat, but did not like them very well; even the Turnips and big Squashes, we thought not so good as our own Squashes and our wild Prairie Turnips.

The government was eager to teach the Indians to raise Potatoes; and to get us women to cultivate them, paid as much as two dollars and a half a day for planting them in the plowed field....

PAWNEE FARMING METHODS

Quite different from the Hopi People of the deserts were the Pawnee People of the Plains. They roamed the land now called Kansas and Nebraska, hunting buffalo. With the coming of horses they became great riders and fought often with their many enemies. They also developed a most spiritual relationship with Nature, frequently expressed in complex ceremonies. These ceremonies took place around several ancient tribal medicine bundles. The chief articles in the large bundles was a pair of corn ears. These were replaced each Fall with a new pair, always grown from the seeds of a stock so ancient and holy that no one was allowed to eat it. The Pawnees grew other kinds of corn for eating.

The Pawnee People combined raising crops with a nomadic life of buffalo hunting. They built large, oval houses of logs, covered with earth. The sunken interior was reached through a doorway large enough to admit horses, which the Pawnees kept indoors for safety. These were their permanent dwellings - always built by a river. The Pawnees had their gardens by these solid homes.

Planting time for the Pawnees began with a very spiritual ground-breaking ceremony, which took place after the first leaves were seen on willows that lined the creeks and rivers. The people waited for the next darkness of Moon, for they had learned that darkness is the time of germination.

The day following the ceremony everyone went to the fields and cleared them of brush and weeds. These were piled and burnt. That night each family took its supply of corn kernels and placed them in a container of water to soak. Some families had special medicine brews that were passed on from generation to generation to help the family's crops grow well.

The next morning came the actual planting. The kernels were kept moist while they were carried to the field. In the field the corn hills were made. First, a buffalo shoulder blade was used as a hoe to break up the soil. Roots were pulled up, remaining weeds were taken away. Then the hills were built up from the surrounding soil. Each family made about twenty hills - spaced two or three feet apart from each other, and two feet or so in diameter, Four to six kernels were planted around the sides of the hill and one on top. The seeds were then covered and the hills shaped into smooth mounds.

The time of corn planting was not long before the people left their earth-lodge villages to roam the Prairies for a Summer of buffalo hunting. Thus, they planted the rest of their crops as soon as the important corn planting was over. Beans were often planted in the same hills as corn - so that the vines could grow up on the corn stalks. Otherwise, willow sticks were used to support the bean vines. The different kinds of corn were separated from each other by patches of pumpkins, squashes and melons. The Pawnee People tried to keep their ten strains of corn pure. The most important divisions of those ten strains were the colours black, white, red and yellow. According to Pawnee creation beliefs, these four colours of corn represent the "four cardinal directions". In the ancient times it was said, there were four villages, each one representing one of the directions. Each of the villages kept one of the colours of corn inside its sacred bundle.

Within the village garden each family had its own plot. This was often fenced with stakes and rawhide ropes, or piles of brush. The plots were from one-half to two acres in size. The gardens were usually located in the moist bottomlands of creeks and rivers. If such a place was very distant from the village, the people sometimes planted a second garden near home.

A day of hard work at planting was followed by a swim in a creek or a sweat bath for men and women. The Pawnees usually built their sweat lodges right inside their spacious earth-covered homes.

It was usually about the first of June when the Pawnee People left their villages. By that time the corn plants were said to be over three feet tall. They were weeded one more time and the hills around them were built up. The people did not come back until about the beginning of September. They buried their valuables and sealed the doors to their earth-lodges with brush. For the Summer they lived in skin tipis, like other buffalo hunting people.

When the people headed back towards their villages with fresh supplies of dried meat and buffalo hides, they sent a party of young men ahead to check things out. The deserted villages were often overrun with fleas so that the people had to keep using their tipis for some time. The young men would return to the main party with news of the village's condition and the success of the crops. Often they would bring along samples of the new corn. A crier was then sent through the tipi camp announcing the news. The people became very anxious to settle back into their solid homes and begin the harvest work. When the condition of the crops had been announced, a joker in the camp might call out: "And how are the Sunflowers growing?" Sunflowers were often planted in the spaces between family plots, where they grew tall and dense. They were favourite places for young Pawnee couples to get acquainted in privacy.

When the Pawnee People first saw their crops again, the corn plants were often ten feet tall, still not fully ripe. They would set up their tipis nearby and then build small shelters of willow right next to the growing crops. Inside the shelters the women would prepare long pits in which they could roast their corn. A fire was built inside the pit and the ears were rested against a log or a small earth bank alongside the pit. The men helped by gathering firewood. If two women were working together, they could roast ears along both sides of the narrow pit. They had to be continually turned to keep them from burning. The ears were roasted until the husks were quite charred, but the kernels were not yet burnt. They were then tossed aside to cool. The husks were left on, to preserve the flavour. After the ears cooled they were husked. Then the women would use a freshwater clam shell and cut the kernels off the cobs, row by row. The kernels were later packed to the camp, where they were spread out on an old lodge cover to dry completely in the sunlight. The children were given pieces of corn stalk to chew on. They would bite into the stalks between the joints and twist them to make the sweet juice come out.

A couple dozen best ears of corn, of the various types, were left whole while the rest were stripped of their kernels. Only the burnt parts of the husks on these ears were removed. The remainder of the husks were peeled back and braided together about a dozen ears at a time. These braided bundles of corn were then hung up to dry. They were kept this way through most of the Winter. It is said that when they were cooked they tasted almost as good as fresh corn on the cob. Sweet corn was preferred fort this kind of preservation.

Often the harvesting was done as a communal affair - two or more families working together to prepare each others crops. It is said that the equivalent of two wagon-loads of corn was prepared in such group efforts during one day, which sometimes lasted far into the night.

It took several days for the scraped corn kernels to dry. Each night they were poured slowly on the old lodge cover, so that the chaff could blow away. The kernels were considered dried when they made tapping noises as they were spilled.

Beans were picked in between the harvests of corn. They were also spread out on old hides and tipi covers to dry by Sunlight. At night they were covered with other hides to keep moisture off. The drying of bean pods was accompanied by popping sounds. After the pods were fairly dry they were beaten with a long, slender willow stick to knock the beans out. Those pods that could not be opened this way were separated by hand. The beans were then poured the same way as corn kernels, to separate them from the pods. Beans were left out in Sunlight for a while longer, until they were thoroughly dry. The Pawnee had eight varieties of beans, which they kept in separate containers.

Pumpkins were harvested next, according to size. The largest ones were brought into camp first. It is estimated that the average family harvested about one and one-half wagon-loads of pumpkins. Back in camp they were roasted in a fire until their outer rind could easily be scraped off with a clam shell. The smallest pumpkins were boiled fresh and eaten during the harvest period. These were about the size of tomatoes. Those that were a little larger were not roasted either. They were just quartered and laid out in Sunlight to dry. Roasted pumpkins were peeled and then cut in half. After the pulp and seeds were removed the halves were cut into slices, like sausages. These sliced pumpkin circles were hung up on a rack to dry. The dry slices were then braided together to form mats about two feet square. These mats could be easily stored. Pieces were cut from them during the Winter, whenever needed.

Various stages of the harvest were taken up by ceremonies with the sacred bundles. Prayers and good thoughts were on the minds of all the people in thanks for having a good food supply for the following seasons. The harvest was completed when the sacred ears of corn were brought from their special plot and exchanged for those that had been inside the sacred bundles during the previous year. These special ears were addressed as Mother Corn. The ceremony of replacement was like a re-charging of the Mother Corn's energies. The old ears were given to distinguished warriors and peace makers to take along on their upcoming expeditions.

When the harvest was over the people moved back into their earth-lodges, having first cleaned and aired them out thoroughly. The next chore consisted of storing away the large quantities of food that had been harvested and dried.

The Pawnee People stored their food in a form of root cellar. It was a round pit, about ten feet deep and about ten feet across at the bottom. The opening, at the top, was much smaller. The bottom of the pit was covered with clean sand. Over this was placed a grating of dry sticks to keep moisture from collecting at the bottoms of the storage bags. The sticks were covered with dry grass, which was usually replaced after each harvest. The walls of the pit were lined with thatch grass which was held in place by the wall shoring of sticks.

The Pawnees used several sizes of storage bags, all of them made from leather. The largest was six feet high and three feet in diameter, when it was full, it was made by sewing two buffalo hides together, folding them, and sewing them again. Inside of these huge bags were stored the kernels scraped from those ears of corn that had matured and dried on the stalks. These were the last ones harvested.

Another large bag stood about three feet high and was about two feet across. In it were stored the dried kernels from the ears that had been roasted. It is said that the bags held about one and a half bushels of corn kernels, each. A smaller bag was about the size of a fifty pound flour sack.

The largest sacks were placed in the bottom of the pit. Their necks were tightly shut and faced inward. The next sized sacks were stacked on top of the first. These were the roasted kernels. They were again faced inward and brought close together, so that the bottoms of the first layer could be seen. As each layer of sacks was put down there resulted a series of steps upon which one could climb down into the pit when it was full. The space in the center of the pit was used to store dried meats and pumpkins and other things that required protection.

An important part of preparing the food storage pit was the closing of it. Enough food was left out to last for about one month at a time. It was thought best not to disturb the storage pits more often than that. Dirt was banked high around the pit entrance, after it had been securely covered. If the pit was not closed properly mice and snakes might enter it easily or moisture might get in and cause the whole supply to become mouldy and useless.

With the ending of the "old days" the people of many tribes learned to grow their own crops and to harvest them. Root cellars were an important part of this new knowledge. Generally these were huge ones built through communal efforts and used by many. Much has been written about early government efforts to interest native people in farming and cultivating. The impression often is that the people were insulted and that those who did make an effort at framing usually failed. That may have been true during a relatively short period of time. Yet, native people of most tribes learned to grow their own vegetables and grains, to keep cows and goats, even to build fine barns, just like any other farmers.

HOPI FARMING METHODS

The Hopi People plant much of their crop on the floodlands along creek and wash bottoms, out in the dry deserts. Alternate sites for fields are usually located at the bottoms of the cliffs which line the edges of valleys, in Hopi country. This is in case the creek bottoms wash out and destroy the crops there. The people learned that plants find moisture at the cliff bottoms, where it seeps down from above. Hopi fields are prepared in February. Brush and weeds are cleared off the plot with a rake made from a sturdy Juniper branch that has three forks. The branch is peeled, the forks are cut to the right length and sharpened, then a cross-piece is tied to them to give added strength. That is the "old way".

Planting is usually done in April. Before that time is held the great Powamu, or Sacred Bean Ceremony. As part of this involved ceremony the Hopi People plant bean and corn seeds in boxes down in the underground Kivas, or Sacred Rooms. Continuous fires turn the Kivas into underground hothouses in which the seeds sprout. If the Kiva crops are successful the people take them as indications of success for the upcoming growing season.

The main tool for planting is a digging stick made of Ironwood or Oak. One end is rounded, the other pointed or wedge-shaped for penetrating the soil. A hole is made a foot or more deep, into which from six to twelve kernels of corn are dropped and covered. Unlike other corn-growing people, those in the Southwest planted their corn below the ground, instead of in hills built up for the purpose. Hills would be more sensitive to winds and lack of water. Husband and wife usually worked together in Hopi planting - the man dug the holes and the woman dropped in the seeds and covered the holes with her feet.

Other vegetable crops were sometimes planted between the rows of corn, or at the edges of corn fields. These included many kinds of beans. One kind, the Scarlet Runner (Phaseolus multiflorus), was grown by the people of South America long before the coming of Columbus. The String Beans are popular with the Hopi because their pods can be eaten. They were the only kinds of beans that the Hopi people dried and stored whole. The others were thrashed at the time of harvesting. The Purple String Bean is the oldest variety among the Hopi.

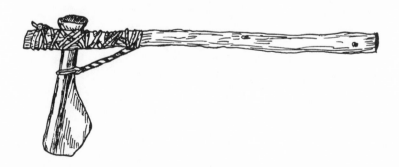

Squashes, melons, and gourds were also planted between the rows of corn, or near them. But more often these crops were planted in separated plots on top of the mesas, closer to the villages. The ancient kind of squash is known as the Striped Cushaw. It was planted in late May or June and harvested after frost. The meat is boiled or baked. The meat was dried for Winter use, also. The shell was cut away and the meat was then sliced in a spiral and wound into long bundles or else the whole squash was sliced up like a sausage and the pieces hung up to dry.

There are many kinds of melons grown by the Hopi. Seeds of those that taste the best are saved and re-planted. Most of these melons come from recently introduced varieties. These taste better than the old-time ones, but they spoil quicker too. The old type of melons could be stored until mid-February. The seeds of melons and squashes were roasted and eaten. They were also crushed and used to oil the stones on which Hopi bread (Piki) was baked.

The Gourd Plant (Lagenaria vulgaris) was grown for functional purposes. Gourds were made into cups, spoons, dippers, canteens, seed bottles, containers for medicines, flutes, trumpets and rattles. Gourd sizes varied. They were planted in weak soil to produce small ones and in good soil for the large.

Peaches are the main fruit crop of the Hopi People, but they also grow apples, apricots, pears, grapes and cherries. The fruit trees are usually planted in the sand dunes under the rocky cliffs. The trees were not usually pruned. Many of today's fruit trees were obtained by the people from nurseries. The fruit harvest is not dependable. It is often destroyed by late frosts and hail storms. The fruits are eaten fresh and dried in great quantity. Peaches, for instance, are split open and spread out in the Sunlight.

Chili Peppers are grown in the irrigated gardens. Often the plants are started indoors and transplanted outdoors after the danger of frost has passed. The peppers are gathered during the season, as they ripen. At Fall frost all the remaining ones are picked. They are strung up and hung in front of the house to dry. More recently introduced varieties have fairly thick skins. These are split and the seeds removed before they are strung to dry.

Some of the ambitious families have made small gardens near Hopi Springs, in recent years. There they grow such vegetables as beets, carrots, cucumbers, lettuce and tomatoes. Sorghum is grown in a few irrigated gardens to provide the people with sweet syrup.

During the Summer the Hopi men and boys tend most of the crops. The women usually tend those that are close to the villages and in need of regular watering. Some men travel many miles in the desert heat in order to keep watch on their fields - especially corn. Even old men usually ran to and from these distant fields.

The people used hoes to clear the weeds from their fields. The blades for the hoes were originally of stone. Later, some were carved from wood. But most commonly they were heavy metal of Spanish manufacture, or from Mexican blacksmiths. After they were available, tin cans were often placed around young plants to protect them from rodents and damage by the Wind. They were also used to make scarecrows.

The tallest Hopi corn grows up to about five feet. many of the ears are harvested and roasted while still green, during the growing season. The rest of the ears are husked and then stored on the cob according to colour. The ears are stacked indoors like firewood. Sometimes they are taken out to be aired and cleaned of dust and insects, during the Winter. The small ears of Sweet Corn used to be baked in pit ovens right out in the fields. Those that survived the feasts which followed the baking were strung up on strands and dried in Sunlight for Winter use. The dried ears were then hung up in the house until needed. The most common and popular type of Hopi corn is a Flour Corn with white kernels. It makes up the main food supply and is one of the most important items in Hopi ceremonies. It is not planted until May or June, and is not harvested until October. Other colours of corn used by the Hopi include blue, red, purple, pink, yellow and violet.

The importance of corn to the Hopi People is summed up in the 1901 statement by an anthropologist named Fewkes:

"Corn is mother in the sense of furnishing sustenance to people who rely upon it for food, and is so highly prized that its seed was committed to the care of the chief of the clan. Every Hopi child has an ear of corn as its special symbolic 'mother'. Every youth initiated into a religious fraternity has a like symbol of his food mother. Each novice at initiation places his special ear of corn on the altar at the time of his introduction into the society."

YUMA GARDENING

The Yuma People in the Southwestern deserts planted their crops according to the Moon and Stars, although the exact details of their systems have never been written down. For instance, they considered the time right for planting when the Pleiades appeared on their Eastern Horizon in the morning, but too late for planting after Orion's Belt showed clearly on the dawning horizon.

Yuma men did most of the planting, using simple hardwood sticks to make holes for the seeds. Typically, the planter poked the stick into the ground several times to make a small circle of loosened earth, which he then scooped out with his hands, leaving a hole four to six inches deep. Seeds were then dropped into this hole (four, ideally, as this was a sacred number) and covered back over with the same soil. Teparies were planted first, then beans, corn and watermelons, finally pumpkins and muskmelons.

Men made the holes, their wives followed with the seeds. Seedlings were not thinned out. Hills and holes were made wherever the soil was easy to work, following no particular pattern or rows. Except for hoeing and weeding once or twice during the growing season, nothing else was done to the plants until harvest time. During weeding, the loose dug-up soil was packed around the plants to help support them and keep them from being blown down by winds.

Hills made for corn were generally about one step apart. Teparies were planted about two feet apart in places where moisture was best, while beans were spaced a bit closer. Pumpkins were kept twelve feet apart, their seeds only two or three inches below the ground, while watermelons were eight feet apart.

Wheat was also planted, but not by the common method of broadcasting the seeds. Instead, they were soaked in water, then placed into circular holes about two inches deep and a foot apart. A pinch of seeds was dropped into each hole, then covered by hand with soil. If successful, it sprouted within days, then grew untended for the season.

Rabbits were a big problem for gardening in the dry desert. Broth in which fish had been cooked was a popular repellent when poured over the plants. Rabbit snares were frequently set up around gardens and baited; some people built low fences around their plants as well.

Small brush was frequently used to keep birds from reaching seeds and seedling. Scarecrows were made to resemble people and often hung with bits of broken pottery.

A popular repellent against insects and small animals was made by collecting the fat from around fish intestines and allowing this to turn ripe in the Sun. The rancid oil was then either wiped around the plants or sprinkled on them with water.

The most successful method of protecting plants was to have boys and young men sleep in the gardens. Tribal ceremonies involving the use of Jimson weed (Datura discolor) were considered essential to obtain successful crops. Similar ceremonies were also held for boys and men before they went hunting and fishing.

A ZUNI CORNFIELD
by Medicine Flower

Medicine Flower, as he was known by his adopted Zuni People, was at first an anthropologist for the Smithsonian Institution. They knew him as Frank Cushing. In the year 1879 they sent him to the Pueblo-dwelling Zuni Tribe on an errand of research. By the time the rest of the research party was ready to return to Washington, D.C. Cushing had become an old Zuni man's adopted son with the name Medicine Flower. Before long he was wearing Zuni clothes, eating Zuni foods, and taking his part in Zuni social and ceremonial affairs. A Zuni headband held back his growing hair.

Medicine Flower wrote a number of stories based on his Zuni Life. A collection of some was published in 1920 by the Museum of the American Indian, in New York, under the title "ZUNI BREADSTUFF". The following words are from that volume.

"My hope has been in so minutely describing these beginnings of a Zuni farm to give a most precious hint to any reader interested in agriculture, or who may possess a field some portions of which are barren because too dry. We may smile at the superstitious observances of the Indian agriculturist, but when we come to learn what he accomplishes, we shall admire and I hope find occasion to imitate his hereditary ingenuity. The country of the Zunis is so desert and dry, that times are of number within even the fickle memory of tradition, the possession of water for drinking and cooking purposes alone has been counted a blessing. Yet, by his system of earth banking, the Zuni Indian and a few of his Western brothers and pupils.... have heretofore been the only human beings who could, without irrigation from living streams, raise to maturity a crop of corn within its parched limits. With the Zunis one-half the months in the year are "nameless", the others are "named". The year is called "a passage of time", the seasons "the steps" (of the year), and the months "crescents" - probably because each begins with the new moon. New Year is called the "midjourney of the sun"; that is, the middle of the solar trip between one summer solstice and another, and, occurring invariably about the nineteenth of December, usually initiates a short season of great religious activity. The first month after this is now called "Growing white crescent".... the month during which "Snow lies not in the pathways".... ends winter....

Spring, called the "Starting time", opens with.... the month of the "Lesser sand storms", followed by.... the month of the "Greater sandstorms".... the ugliest season of the Zuni year.... Summer and autumn, the period of the "months nameless", are together called.... "Bringing flour-like clouds". In priestly or ritualistic language these six months, although called nameless, are designated successively the "yellow, blue, red, white, variegated or iridescent, and black", after colours of the plumed prayer-sticks sacrificed in rotation at the gull of each moon to the gods of the North, West, South, East, the skies and the lower regions respectively.

Early in the month of the "Lesser sandstorms", the same Zuni, we will say, who preempted, a year since, a distant arroyo-field, goes forth, hoe and axe in hand, to resume the work of clearing, etc. Within the sand embankment he now selects that portion which the arroyo enters from above, and cutting many forked cedar branches, drives them firmly into the dry stream-bed, in a line crossing its course, and extending a considerable distance beyond either bank. Against this row of stakes he places boughs, clods and rocks, sticks, and earth, so as to form a strong barrier or dry-dam; open, however, at either end. Some rods below this on either side of the stream-course, he constructs, less carefully, other and longer barriers. Still farther down, he seeks in the "tracks" of some former torrent, a ball of clay, which, having been detached from its native bank, far above, has been rolled and washed, down and sown, ever growing rounder and smaller and tougher, until in these lower plains it lies embedded in and baked by the burning sands. This he carefully takes up, breathing reverently from it, and places it on ones side of the stream-bed, where it is desirable to have the rain-freshlets overflow. He buries it, with a brief supplication, in the soil, and then proceeds to heap over it a solid bank of earth which he extends obliquely across, and to some distance beyond the arroyo. Returning, he continues the embankment past the clay ball either in line of, or at whatever angle with the completed portion seems to his practised eye most suited to the topography.

The use of the principle barriers and embankments may be inferred from the terms of the invocation with which the field is consecrated after the completion of all the earth-works. The owner then applies to whatever corn-priest is keeper of the sacred "medicine" of his clan or order. This priest cuts and decorates a little stick of red willow with plumes from the legs and hips of the eagle, turkey and duck, and with the tail-feathers from the Maximilian's Jay, nighthawk, yellow-finch, and ground sparrow, fastening them on, one over the other, with cords of fine cotton. From the store of paint which native tradition claims was brought from the original birthplace of the nation, he takes a tiny particle, leavening it with a quantity of black mineral powder. To a sufficient measure of rainwater he adds a drop of ocean water with which he moistens the pigment, and with a brush made by chewing the end of a yucca leaf, applies the point to the stick. With the same paint he also decorated s section of cane filled

with wild tobacco supposed to have been planted by rain, hence sacred. These two objects, sanctified by his breath, he gives to the applicant. Taking them carefully in his left hand, the latter goes forth to his new field. Seeking a point in the middle of the arroyo below his earthworks, he kneels, or sits down on hide blanket, facing East. He then lights his cane cigarette, and blows smoke toward the North, West, South, East, the upper and the lower regions. Then holding the smoking stump and the plumed prayer stick near his breast, he says a prayer. From the substance of his prayer which.... We find he believes that: He has infused the consciousness of his prayer into the plumed stick; that with his sacred cigarette he has prepared a way "like the trails of the winds and rains" (clouds) for the wafting of that prayer to the gods of all regions. That, having taken the cloud-inspiring down of the turkey, the strength giving plume of the eagle, the water-loving feather of the duck, the path-finding tails of the birds who counsel and guide the Summer; having moreover severed and brought hither the flesh of the water-attracting tree, which he has dipped the god-denizened ocean beautified with the very cinders of creation, bound with strands from the dress of the skyborn goddess of cotton · he beseeches the god-priests of the earth, sky, and cavern, the beloved gods whose dwelling places are in the great embracing waters of the world, not to withhold their mist-laden breaths, but to canopy the earth with cloud banners, and let fly their shafts little and mighty of rain, to send forth the fiery spirits of lightning, lift up the voice of thunder echoes shall step from mountain to mountain, bidding the mesas shake down streamlets. The streamlets shall yield torrents; the torrents, foam-capped, soil laden, shall boil toward the shrine he is making, drop hither and thither the soil they are bearing, leap over his barricades unburdened and stronger, and in place of their lading, bear out toward the ocean as payment and faith-gift the smoke-cane and the prayer-plume...."

CHIPPEWA GARDEN VILLAGE

Told by Nodinens (Little Wind) Age 74

(Excerpt from: Densmore, Frances **CHIPPEWA CUSTOMS**)

"The six families went together, and the distance was not long. Each family had a large bark house with a platform along each side, like the lodge in which the maple sap was boiled. We renewed the bark if necessary, and this was our summer home."

"The camps extended along the lake shore, and each family had its own garden. We added to our garden every year, my father and brothers breaking the ground with old axes, bones, or anything that would cut and break up the ground. My father had wooden hoes that he made, and sometimes we used the shoulder blade of a large deer or a moose, holding it in the hand."

"We planted potatoes, corn and pumpkins. These were the principal crops. After the garden was planted the Mide gathered together, made a feast, and asked the Mide manido to bless the garden. They had a kind of ceremony and sang Mide songs. Old women could attend this feast, but no young people were allowed. Children were afraid when their parents told them to keep away from such a place. The gardens were never watered. A scarecrow made of straw was always put in a garden."

"In the Spring we had pigeons to eat. They came in flocks and the men put up long fish nets on poles, just the same as in the water, and caught the pigeons that way. We boiled them with potatoes and meat. We went to get wild potatoes in the spring and a little later the blueberries, gooseberries, and June berries were ripe along the lake shore. The previous fall the women had tied green rice in long bundles and at this time they took it out, parched and pounded it, and we had that for food. There was scarcely an idle person around the place."

"The women made cedar-bark mats and bags for summer use. By that time the reeds for making floor mats were ready for use. They grew in a certain place and the girls carried them to the camp. We gathered plenty of the basswood bark and birch bark, using our canoes along the lake and the streams. We dried berries and put them in bags for winter use. During the summer we frequently slept in the open.

"Next came the rice season. The rice fields were quite a distance away and we went there and camped while we gathered rice. Then we returned to our summer camp and harvested our potatoes, corn, pumpkins, and squash, putting them in caches which were not far from the gardens.

"By this time the men had gone away for the fall trapping. When the harvest was over and colder weather came, the women began their fall fishing, often working at this until after the snow came. When the men returned from the fall trapping we started for the winter camp."

BLACKFOOT NAMES FOR BIRDS AND ANIMALS

Schools and classrooms of the Past were outdoors, in Nature. Blackfoot children grew up seeing wild birds, plants and animals as a modern child grows up with radios, magazines and grocery stores. Those who were especially interested in learning about their environment usually grew up to become healers and ceremonial leaders, wise persons who were consulted on all manner of daily things; gifts and payments were usually presented for their knowledge and advice.

Because birds and animals are frequently addressed in traditional Blackfoot prayers (along with other elements of Nature), missionaries and others often thought the people were so naive as to think of these creatures as "gods". They called Indians "heathens", meaning without real religion, and said they practised "animism". Actually, prayers about birds, animals and so forth are addressed to the "spirits" of these creatures, which are thought to be in closer contact with the Creator than any living beings.

Until the coming of trappers and traders, Blackfoot hunters seldom killed anything they could not use completely. Yet, it cannot be said that they never did so. For instance, the ancient tribal way of getting buffalo was to lure them near steep cliffs, then drive them over the side to be killed or maimed by the fall. Such a place was called a "piskan". Since this method was not very controlled, often more buffalo went over than the people could use. A hunter who got more meat and hides than he could handle made a prayer to the Sun, explaining the situation and leaving the excess as an "offering" for other beasts.

Blackfoot names in the following lists are intended to give the reader a "feel" for the native language. Blackfoot is hard to speak and harder to write, since it only developed orally. Blackfoot readers should consult with teachers and family elders for correct pronunciations; approximate translations are given in English for all others.

BIRDS

BIRD: The general word for bird is piksi whose meaning has been lost in time. Small birds are sistsi; very small birds are poksistsi. **EAGLE:** Pitai is the golden eagle, whose feathers are used for headdresses and other ceremonial purposes. Ksikichkinni means "white head" the bald eagle, whose feathers are seldom used. **HAWK:** The hawks as a group are called aiinnimaiaks, or "siezers". The large rough-legged hawk is ishpochsoatsis, or "used as a tailfeather", because its tailfeathers resemble those of the golden eagle (except smaller), and are sometimes used as substitutes. The little sparrow hawk is called pispski, meaning something about "very high", while the sharp-shinned hawk is called omachk-pipski or "big very high". The osprey is known as pachtsik-sistsikum, or "mistaken for thunder", because of the noise its feathers make when it dives from the sky. **OWL:** Called sepisto, or "night crier". The big-horned owl is called kakonotstoki, or "hollow ear". **SWAN:** Ksikomachkaii, or "white going home", because it was usually seen in Blackfoot country only while mig-

rating. **GOOSE:** The Canadian goose is called apspini or "white cheeks", while the snow goose is einoch-ksikanikim, or dark-tipped feathers. **DUCK:** Sa-aeh is the common name. Each kind of duck also has its own name, such as Meksikatsi, or "red feet". **PELICAN:** Sochkaukumi, or "big throat". **GREBE:** Meek-sistayeeh, "red diver", because of the graceful way it goes under water. **LOON:** Matsiisaipi, or "handsome charger", because of the way it skims across water, like a proud warrior going into battle. **RAVEN:** Omachkaisto, or "big crow". Considered the wisest of birds, often watched for signs. Warriors tried to follow their flight, in search of success; two ravens close together, however, were thought to mean they had secrets to discuss about some pending misfortune, causing warriors to turn back. A lone raven circling over camp meant news was coming. **WOODPECKER:** Pachpakskskissi, or "pounding its nose". The red-headed woodpecker, whose cry sounds somewhat like the Blackfoot expression, "stick your heads out so that I can eat you," is mikimita, which means "fire-reddened breast", or ekotsotokan, which means "red head". **MAGPIE:**Mamiatsikim, or "has a body like a fish", because of its long tail. Its cry resembles a slumber song old Blackfoot women sing for little children: "Long tails, fly ahead and stab your provision bag at my door." It refers to the way they stab their beaks at whatever they can find. **MEADOWLARK:** Otachkuikaii, or "yellow breast". Another name is Soch-ksee-simstahn, or "hollowed-like-a-rectum", because of the shape of its nest! The arrival back of meadowlarks meant spring had come. Their presence around tipi camps meant all was well and peaceful. **KINGBIRD:** Sikiminiwanyeh, or "stingy with berries", because it makes a great ruckus if anyone comes to pick berries near where it is feeding. **WATER OUZEL:** Ikisisakum, or "meat"; it will dip its head in response to hearing this name called aloud. **ROCKY MOUNTAIN JAY:** Apiakunski, or "white forehead". **STELLAR'S JAY:** Omachkutskuisistsi, or "big blue bird". **WAXWING:** Simitsima, or "Main lodge pole", for the appearance of the pointed crest on its head. **GROUSE:** Kitssitsum, or "looking like smoke". The Franklin grouse is called matsapsi kitssitsum, or "crazy looking like smoke", because it is so stupid that it can be approached and killed with a stick. In English, this one is called "fool hen".

ANIMALS

DOG: Imitai, an ancient word whose meaning has been lost. The average Blackfoot family had about twelve dogs, before the coming of horses. These were used mainly to help move the household from one campsite to the next, and to a much lesser extent for hunting and guarding. Even with their packs and travois, these big wolf-like animals would frequently fight, chase wild beasts, or run into water. **HORSE:** The first horses seen by Blackfeet looked like elk but were used like dogs, thus they were named ponokamita, or "elk dog". Towards the mid-1700's their arrival quickly changed the whole Blackfoot way of life, as the automobile has done to modern people. Hunting and camp moving became much easier, and warfare more common, with horses the main prizes of intertribal raiding. The average family needed eight or ten horses, though a few owned herds of several hundred. These were the small and hardy "Indian ponies", which are about extinct today after years of govern ment effort to replace them with larger "white man's horses" for ranch and farm use. **BUFFALO:** Einiua, which is said to refer to the animal's black horns, although exact meaning of the name has been forgotten. A list of traditional uses for buffalo parts is long, including meat and various intestines for eating, plus hides for lodge covers, clothing, robes, containers and so forth. Buffalo are still very important to Blackfoot traditional ceremonies, although beef parts are usually used as substitutes. **ELK:** Called Ponakau, having to do with the animal's long legs. They were hunted especially when buffalo could not be found, all parts of them being useful to traditional life. Every elk has two canine teeth which are like Blackfoot pearls or diamonds, the most valuable decorations for dresses and necklaces.

O.H.W.

O.H.W.

MOOSE: Sixtisoo, meaning something like "black charging through", because of their dark bodies and the way they travel through thick brush and deep swamps. Hunted and used like elk, though not very common in Blackfoot country. Bowls were frequently made from their flat antlers. **WHITE-TAILED DEER:** Auwahtuye, or "waving the tail from side to side". **MULE DEER:** Issikotuye, or "black-tipped-tail". **ANTELOPE:** Saki-au-wakahsi, or "white big horn". Wild goats and sheep were hunted mainly for their hides, since it was difficult to travel in their domain. **CARIBOU:** Omachtsistsini, or "big hoof", an animal seldom seen or hunted because of its rugged mountain domain. **BEAR:** Kiyaio, a name referring to the animal's head and neck. Sikoch-kiyaio is literally the "black bear", while Omachka-kiyaio is the "big bear", or grizzly. Only the bravest men would hunt or attack these animals, and only they were allowed to wear its claws. Bear meat was not eaten, and other body parts were only used for ceremonial purposes. **COYOTE:** Ksino-au, referring to the way they sneak around without being seen. This name is mainly for the small prairie coyote. Another name is Apeesee, said to connote the distant relationship with dogs. This is mainly for the larger coyote, also known as the bush wolf. **WOLF:** Makwi, referring to one who gets and eats plenty. Another name is Omachkapeesee, or "big wolf". **BOBCAT:** Atayo, referring to the animal's scream; also known as Suapit, or "fringes on the legs". **LYNX:** Sok-atayo, or "heavy bobcat". **MOUNTAIN LION:** Omachk-atayo, or "big bobcat". **KIT FOX:** Sinopah, meaning something like "he has arrows"; this suggests the fox's ability to strike swiftly and unexpectedly. **RED FOX:** Otatoye; means something like "distant Medicine robe", referring to an ancient custom of using a red fox skin in place of cloth for making an offering to Sun. **WOLVERINE:** Issistsi, meaning either "claws shaped like hooves", or "carrying its young". **FISHER:** Pinutuye, referring to the way the hair on its tail stands straight out as though it had been clipped.

OTTER: Emonissi, referring to the way it slides around and is difficult to approach when on land. **BEAVER:** Ksisstukki, meaning something like "cutting trees with its teeth". Beaver skins made popular winter clothing long ago, because the hair is good at shedding water and snow. **MUSKRAT:** Misochpski, or "hard-puffed face". **MARTEN:** Asinnatuye, which means something like "young cropped tail", or in other words, "young fisher". **WEASEL:** Otao is the summer weasel, referring to its brown coat. The winter weasel, or ermine, is called Apao, referring to its white coat. The winter skin of white with a black tip is symbolic of life and death, along with other things, in Blackfoot tradition. For that reason, weasel skins were favoured for decorating all sorts of things, including sacred headdresses and ceremonial suits, each accompanied by weasel-ceremony transfers. Weasels were snared with sinew loops. Their skin was peeled off, stretched with a willow stick, and left to dry. It was then tanned by vigorous rubbing between the hands until it got soft. **BLACKFOOT FERRET:** Omach-apao, or "big weasel", since it looks similar to the ermine. **MINK:** Soyekaye, meaning something like "wet back" or "water on its back". **SKUNK:** Apikayi, or "white along its back". **RACCOON:** Siksikishzep-ototoye, or "black-striped red fox". **BADGER:** Misinskiyo, meaning something like "sharply pointed nose". **PORCUPINE:** Kaiskachp, referring to the way it bristles its quills when threatened. These animals served as emergency food, especially for men on the warpath who had lost their weapons. Porcupines do not run away, so they can be clubbed with a stick. The tails were used as hair brushes. **RABBIT:** Ahtsista, referring to the way this animal crouches down with its hind legs. Mistaki-ahtsista, is the "Mountain", or Snowshoe Rabbit. Sik-ahtsista means "black rabbit", and refers to the Cottontail. **PRAIRIE DOG:** Omachk-okatta. The first part means "big", the second refers to the way these animals were captured by children. A loop of sinew laid over the animal's hole snared it when it stuck out its head. The same name now also refers to gophers. **MARMOT:** Omachk-sikitsis-omachk-okatta, meaning something like "big- toothed, big-snared". **MOUSE:** Kahnes-skiena, meaning something like "old face". **WOOD RAT:** Omachs-kahnes-skiena, or "big mouse". **SHREW:** Pokok-kaisksisi-kahnes-skiena, or "small, long-pointed-nosed mouse". **CHIPMUNK:** Miatsikaye, or "striped back". **SQUIRREL:** Eekaiiseah, referring to the animal's warning cry. **FLYING SQUIRREL:** Apastoksi-eekaiiseah, or "white-faced squirrel". **BAT:** Motaienstami, meaning something like "owner of many lodge poles". When a bat's wings are spread out, they look like lodge covers with many lodge poles, or small bones, underneath.

HUNTING

"Before I go out to look for a deer, I always pray first and burn incense," said a tribal elder who spent his whole life in the shadows of the Rockies. "I call on the deer's spirit and tell it that I'm not coming with mean intentions. I tell it that I'm sorry to take its life, but that I need the meat for my family."

That is the basis of understanding native hunting techniques. A great deal of skill is involved - a lifetime of training - but it only works properly when combined with a spiritual attitude of deep respect for the animal and its home in nature, and for the Creator who made it all.

Trophy hunting was not practised at all by the native people, who killed animals only for food and other practical reasons. The oldest and largest of a breed were generally not disturbed; considered wisest, they were left to pass on their strengths through mating. Besides, their meat was often very tough.

In native culture there is a use for every part of a slain animal, including meat, organs and intestines for food, hides for dwellings and clothing, horns for cups and bowls, even the hooves for making glue. But that is not to say that nothing was ever wasted, as some idealists have claimed. When storage and transportation was limited, it was not always practical to take everything from a slain animal. The important factor is that it was always treated with respect; if parts were left behind, the hunter said a prayer of thanks, in which he offered the remnants to other spirits in nature who would make use of them.

Hunting with home-made bows and arrows requires patience, skill and an intimate knowledge of nature. With hungry families waiting anxiously at home, traditional hunters had a much different outlook on their work than modern sportsmen. The introduction of firearms changed this kind of work tremendously; gunshots disturb nature as if one had shouted loudly, "Shut up!" No one who truly loves nature can enjoy making such a disturbance, even when it's needed to obtain family food.

Trapping and snaring are ancient ways of obtaining wild foods silently. However, the miseries they cause to wildlife make their use unpopular with ever-growing numbers of people. Steel traps are specially cruel, causing many animals to die slowly of torture. Primitive people had to rely on traps and snares not only for food, but also for furs to make clothing and bedding. However, the mass killing of animals for furs to be sold was unknown.

A ZUNI HUNT

(Excerpt from: Cushing, Frank Hamilton **ZUNI BREADSTUFF**)

Few among ourselves can realize how simply the Southwestern Indian is able to travel the wilds which surround his desert home. ....His requirements are insignificant compared with what we have learned to regard as essential to the traveler's barest needs.... A bag of 'tchu-ki-na-o-we', another of coarse meal, and a saddle-wallet of dried 'he-we', complete, if we but add salt, red pepper, and tobacco in smaller sacks.... These, together with a small bowl and a little cooking pot, he rolls up in a blanket and mounts on the rear of his saddle, to the bow of which he also slings a bottle of water-tight wickerware. Underneath that saddle, as a sort of padding, are a thick cloth and half of a deerskin dressed soft with the hair on. Over his shoulders is strapped a quiver and bow-case, slung to his side a hunting knife, and about his waist is ingeniously twirled his heavy serape - overcoat, waterproof, and bed-covering combined; for the skin and cloth under the saddle, and the blanket in which are enwrapped his utensils and provisions, serve with cedar-twigs or a few handfuls of grass, for his bed.

It was in the early years of my life at Zuni that Pa-lo-wah-ti-wa, a young half-brother named Kesh-pa-he, and I set out one sandy morning for the far-away southern mesas.... All day long, never stopping for rest or refreshment, we kept on our course. Growing thirsty, I was advised to pick gum from the pine shrubs we passed under, and by chewing it allay my longing for water....

From the wooded, hilly mesa-tops we descended, just as the Sun was setting, into one of those long, low, white-walled canyons south of Zuni.... No sooner were we well down before an exclamation from Pa-lo-wah-ti-wa caused me to look around. "Supper is ready!" he cried, pointing to a little cottontail rabbit which was just scudding into a hole in the rocks. Forthwith Kesh-pa-he dismounted, and cutting a slender twig, so trimmed the branches from it as to leave one or two hooks or barbs at the lower end. He then pushed the twig into the hole, prodded about until he suddenly exclaimed, 'There he is!', then began to twist the twig until it would no longer turn about, when, giving it a cautious pull, behold! out came the rabbit, as thoroughly fastened to the end of the rod as though transfixed by a spear.... Before he was fairly dead, the Indians drew his face up to their own and breathed from his nostrils the last faint sighs of his expiring breath....

....They built a fire....when the horses had been brought back and hobbled, and the snow collected on a blanket out of range of the heat, one of the Indians found a flat stone and three or four lesser ones.... The flat stone was mounted on the others as a table on very short legs, so propped up at one end, however, that it sloped gently from the fire near which it was stationed. Under the end opposite the fire our one bowl was placed, and on the flat rock the snow was heaped....as high as it could be packed.... In a few moments the snow began to melt very rapidly, and the water....ran a constant stream into the bowl.

The Indians now began to prepare our first meal. One of the rabbits they threw into the middle of the blazing fire, where almost instantly the hair and parts of the skin were singed off. When the carcass looked more like a cinder than the body of an animal, it was hauled forth, and....divested of its charred skin as a nut would be of its shuck - then dressed, spread out on a skewer, spitted and set up slantingly, to take care of itself for a while before a thick bed of embers.

From the basket-bottle some water was poured into our cooking pot, and when it had begun to boil violently, some coarse meal was briskly stirred in. Before this had quite become mush, while still sticky and quite thin, that is, some of it was poured out on a stone, some dry meal thoroughly kneaded into it, and the whole ingeniously wrapped or plastered around the end of a long stick. This stick, like the rabbit spit, was then set up slantingly over the coals and occasionally turned until considerably swollen, and browned to a nicety. Behold a fine loaf of....exceedingly good-tasting cornbread!

The bowl of snow-water was removed from its place under the stone, and into it was stirred some 'tchuk-ki-na-o-we' - just enough to make a cream-like fluid to serve as our beverage, and on the upturned sides of our saddle skins, in the light and warmth of our genial fire, our meal was at last spread out....

And now, after the food was disposed of, the ashes were raked away from where our first fire had been built.... The sand underneath was dry as dust and hot, but not enough so to scorch the thin layer of cedar twigs with which each of our hastily scooped out hip-holes was speedily lined.

Over the cedar leaves we spread the saddle-cloths and skins, over these our wrapping-blankets and serapes. A few more logs were brought in and placed near the fire, a little shelter of cedar branches built to keep the wind off our heads, then we stretched out to smoke our cigarettes, listen to the hunter-tales of our elder brother, and to make plans for the morrow's hunting."

A HIDATSA WINTER HUNT

Told by Wolf-Chief

The following story was told to Gilbert Wilson and his brother Frederick in 1911. Wolf-Chief was an old and renowned Hidatsa man. The Hidatsa were people of the Plains, living in the area of present-day North Dakota. They lived in tipis while roaming after herds of buffalo. However, much of the year was spent in circular houses made of logs and earth, near which they had large gardens.

The Wilson brothers stayed with the Hidatsa People one or two months each year from 1908 to 1918, recording and sketching the "old ways". They were adopted by Buffalobird Woman, whose brother was Wolf- Chief. This his story. "In the spring of 1866, when we were living in Like-a-fish-hook village and I was about seventeen years old, my father, Small-ankle, invited me to go with him to Little Knife Creek to hunt beaver.... Our five villages once stood at the mouth of Knife River.

We saddled two horses for mounts and in addition took three extra horses, one of them saddled with a flat saddle, as he was a buffalo horse, a racer. My father rode ahead and led one horse; I followed, also mounted, and drove the two remaining horses before me. Four of our horses bore frame saddles of horns of white-tailed deer. Such saddles were considered better than those of wood, since they did not gall the horse's back.... Our extra horses were not loaded.

Tied to the rear of the saddle that Small-ankle rode were two steel traps with the chains tied together and wrapped in a piece of tent skin. He had rolled up two pieces of tent skin and had laid them behind my saddle and bound them to my saddle horn. My father and I each had two robes. I doubled one of my robes, flesh side up, and threw it over my saddle; my father did likewise. As we rode, we each wore a new robe, fur side in, belted about the body.

We had one dog and travois and on the travois we carried a small hatchet, a hoe, and a small brass kettle, also some parched corn balls and pounded parched corn for mush. All these we wrapped up in some canvas we obtained from the soldiers.

....The dog followed along in the rear. ....We did not travel very fast. We knew the place we were going to was only about forty miles from Like-a-fish-hook village and we could reach it before sunset....(of the second day).

My father had a muzzle-loading flintlock and I had a short-barrelled percussion rifle and my bow and arrows. My bow was of elm wood and I carried eighteen iron-headed and four blunt-headed arrows in my quiver. We still used arrows at that time. We used our guns in battle with our enemies and to kill deer and antelope; but powder was scarce and not much used in hunting buffalo.

(Excerpt from: Wilson, Gilbert Livingstone
THE HORSE AND DOG IN HIDATSA CULTURE)

O.H.W.

We reached the camping place and dismounted. My father untied our dog from the travois. He was a good dog and not very tired. As soon as the travois was removed he rolled in the snow, getting up and shaking his hide, but not barking. We also unloaded our horses, but did not hobble them. "They are tired and will not stray far," said my father. We had made about twenty miles that day.

Our horses attended to, my father began putting up the frame of our tent. He raised the travois, stayed it against a forked pole, and against these leaned other poles, which he brought from the timber.... It was about six feet high.... It was covered with three pieces of old tent skin, two at the front and one at the back. My father pierced holes in the skins with his knife and through the holes drew thongs to lace the skins together....

My father soon returned. "I have a fat badger," he said. He dressed it, made a fire, put the meat into our kettle and added some mint blossoms and chokecherry bark which he had gathered when he was hunting the badger. "They will give a fragrant smell to the mess," he said. He boiled the meat in water from the creek; when it was boiled, he threw out the water   and added fresh water. Badger flesh is rather strong and must be parboiled....

We went to bed, my father on the north side of the tent; I on the south. My dog slept at my side. Our saddles were laid against the wall. In this case, we did not use tent pins or stones to hold down the edge of the covering; it merely hung to the ground. The floor of our tent had been scraped free of snow with our hoe.... "Put your gun beside you," my father had said to me. "If enemies fire at our tent, pay no attention to anything, but seize your gun." I laid my gun between myself and the skin covering of the tent with the barrel pointing in the same direction as my head. We had a small fire outside our tent. We carried with us one drinking cup.

We remained at this place all the next day. My father went afoot up the river to look for game. He found a pile of bones left by a party who had killed buffalo; and brought back as many of them as he could carry, as they were fresh and had not spoiled in the cold weather.... He went outside the tent and pounded the bones with our hatchet and cut them up. "I have found a great deal of grease," he said. He meant, of course, that the bones were rich in grease. "Short distance from here, I found something very good to eat," my father said, as he showed me some kind of a mushroom which we call....wood....navel.

After taking out the bones, my father put the mushrooms in the broth and boiled them. They were very good and tasted something like squash. I had never eaten them before and never since then. I do not know whether my father learned of their use from white men or Indians....

My eyes hurt for three days. My father dropped some gunpowder in my eyes to cool them. Snowblindness sometimes turns the eyeball white. "If after you are well," Small-ankle said, "we find a white spot on your eyeball we will chew a piece of straight sage leaf mixed with charcoal and slip it into the eye. This will remove the white spot." I have heard of this remedy from other members of our tribe.... The gunpowder hurt my eyes a little, but felt cool, nevertheless. My father wet a little on his palm, I lay on my back and opened my eyes and he dropped a little of the wet gunpowder on my eyeball.

We stayed in this camp for three days and then moved up the river about fifteen miles, to some small timber in a coulee. As we approached the timber I saw something move and called to my father, "What is ahead of us?" "A porcupine," he answered.... It was going rather fast. "Let us camp here," said my father, "and we will have porcupine for supper." We dismounted. My father cut a stick and killed the porcupine. When a porcupine is frightened he tries to hide in the bushes. My father struck the porcupine on the head; he dragged the animal to camp, holding it by a foreleg to avoid the spines. "Make a fire and burn off all the hairs and quills, and we will eat the skin,' he said.

I built a fire and held the porcupine over the coals. When the quills were all singed, I scraped them off with a stick. I opened the belly and skinned the animal, leaving all the fat and some of the meat on the skin. I took off the skin and fats and adhering flesh, but without any bones clinging to it. I roasted this fat skin. I cut a green stick forked at one end in three tines like a white man's fork. On these I laid the porcupine skin and held it over the fire. After the entrails were removed the rest of the carcass was broiled.... I called out to him, "This fat skin is done." The porcupine skin had been taken off in two pieces, one piece from each side; but I had broiled only one piece which I laid on the grass. It was very good, quite fat and very tasty....

The next day we started back to Spring Creek. The ice on the river was not yet broken and though we had seen some beaver dams we had killed no beavers. However, we discovered a herd of five buffalo bulls on our way. "I want to give chase to those buffaloes," I said to Small-ankle. "Good," he answered, "but you had better take your gun. I fear you are hardly strong enough in your arm to use arrows." "Yes I am," I said. "Have you not heard that I have already killed a grown buffalo with an arrow?" "I think you should take your gun," said my father, "but use your arrows if you will. Now let me tell you again how to judge if one of the bulls is fat. As you come close, observe if the hair along the spine and just back of the eyes is black. Those so marked are the fat ones."

The reason of this is that the black hair marked where the buffalo had

begun to shed his hair. Under the black spots were layers of fat that in these places made the buffalo shed a little earlier than his leaner fellows. But such a sign was of value only in the spring and was found only on bulls, not on cows.

I mounted my horse, a large gray one without saddle. I wore a coat made of a white wool blanket, bound about with a belt. I tied my quiver to the left side of my belt, and gave chase to the herd. Observing one with the signs my father head described, I singled him out, and soon caught up with him. Coming very close and knowing just where to shoot, I released my arrow. It sunk in half its length. I followed a little way until I saw blood gush out of the buffalo's mouth. Then I reined in.

The buffalo slowed down, stopped, and stood swaying. More blood flowed from his mouth and his forelegs bent under him. He tried to rise, sank again; tried once more to rise, but could not, and fell over on his side, dead.

He lay on his left side, with my arrow sticking out of his right. I thought to get my arrow, then said to myself, "No, I will bring my father here and show him how I can kill a buffalo with an arrow."....

I led his horse, both of us mounted; my father had covered his eyes, as they pained him greatly. Snowblindness was a common trouble with us in the spring.

We came to the dead buffalo. "There," I exclaimed, "see that!" My father uncovered his eyes a little and saw the buffalo. He put his hand to his mouth in astonishment. "You have shot it just like a man," he cried. "Now sit down and rest yourself and I will dress the carcass for you. This is the fattest bull I ever saw." He knew the bull was fat from its looks.

My father skinned the bull, cut out the meat for drying, and laid the pieces on the sod where the snow had melted and left the ground bare. When he had done he opened the belly and pulled out the intestines and paunch. In the cavity of the body was now some warm blood.

"I want to drink some of this blood," said my father. He filled his joined palms and drank two or three times. "You do likewise, my son," he said to me. "If you are going to eat the fresh liver and kidneys and that part of the paunch" - (he meant the part that is filled with thin stuff like leaves) - "you should first drink a little blood. It will save you from getting sick in the stomach."

I drank some of the blood, but did not like it. "You need not drink much," said Small-ankle. "You have drunk enough to keep the raw liver from hurting you."

We camped at night on a hill and Small-ankle made bone grease. A storm came up and it began to snow. "We must move our camp down into the timber," said my father. "Our tent may blow over up here." The next day we moved our tent down in a coulee out of the wind and pitched it in a place near a big tree where it was protected by some bushes. It snowed all day. In the evening it was still snowing, but we went back to our meat pile near our former camp on the hill to take our meat back to our tent. Snow was still falling when we went to bed. I slept that night on the west side with my head toward the rear of the tent. The tent door was toward the south.

Our tent poles were small and not heavy enough to support the weight of the snow. I do not know how it happened, but apparently the snow on the side of the hill above us on the west drifted and came down upon me. My father awoke during the night to find the tent giving way and weighted down with snow. The space inside the tent was reduced almost to nothing. He sprang across and found me under the snow, unconscious. He carried me to the farther side of the tent, sang a mystery song, and felt my heart. Like one in a dream, I heard him singing. Gradually my senses returned. "Are you alive again!" cried my father. "Yes," I answered, my breath coming in gasps, as I sat up.

My father held me in his arms, as I sat on the ground, but I was able to sit upright only by leaning my head against the tent wall. The wall was icy cold, but I could not sit up otherwise. "I once heard," said my father, "of a tent being covered with snow. The people inside hit the walls of the tent with their hands and kept the snow from crushing it to the ground.

He struck the tent wall repeatedly at one side, driving back the snow and packing it; after a while he had quite a space cleared. "You sit here," my father said. I moved over to the side where he had been working and he attacked the other side of the tent. At last, he had the tent restored to something like its normal shape.

I suppose I had been pressed down with the snow and was dead (fainted). As I have said, my father felt with his hand and felt my heart beat. He put water on my face and sang mystery songs until I revived. In the meantime my dog was running around overhead.

"Father, I am hungry," I said. "I don't wonder," answered my father, "I think we have been here for three days. You ought to be hungry." He took two boiled buffalo tongues and one buffalo heart from a bag which lay on his pillow. We ate all the meat, for we were hungry. I felt my face and hands and said, "Father, I am well now." "Good," he said, "let us try to

71

find our hoe. I laid it just outside the door." We both worked at the door, pushing and shaking it until finally my father worked his way out and I heard him cry, "I have found it." I still felt very weak. All this time our breath froze as soon as it struck the cold air. There was no fire in the tent and I found that the hood that formed part of my coat was torn off at the neck. Doubtless, it had frozen to the ground and had been torn off when my father pulled me from my bed. My father had just found the hoe when suddenly we saw light above. Before this it had been quite dark. It looked as if the snow up there was not very deep. "I will try to push a hole through that place," said my father. He pulled a buck brush from his bed and tearing off a piece of his shirt, he bound several of the buck brush sticks together, reached up, and punched a hole in the snow above the smoke hole of the skin tent. We saw that it was daylight and the snow was still falling. The air coming down the smoke hole made me chilly.

My father now dug with the hoe into the snow at the door and as he dug I kept shoving the snow back into the lodge. We both wore our mittens, but my father covered his head with a saddle skin set over his hair like a cap. He cut holes in the edges of the saddle skin where they overlapped and stuck a stick through to skewer the edges together. This saddle skin cap prevent the snow from falling on his bare head, as he was digging a tunnel through the snowdrift. He had tunnelled for a distance of about twelve feet when he said, "my knees are very cold, will you try to help me?" I put on his cap and went to work. I threw the loose snow back into the lodge, quite filling it. We continued to work in this manner and finally broke through the drift about eighteen feet from the tent. We had worked on our knees and dug a tunnel high enough to kneel in; the snow was at least ten feet deep. The mouth of the tunnel was about eighteen feet from the lodge and breast high from the ground, for we found that we had not tunnelled along on top of the ground at all.

When I finally reached the outer air I found that the day was quite pleasant and not very cold. We had noticed geese going northwest before the storm came up. As my feet touched the ground, I shouted "Good," and as my father appeared, I cried out to him, "I see only the head and shoulders of our race horse." "That is unfortunate," answered my father, "perhaps the other hoses have perished.

Small-ankle and I dug the horse out with our hoe. When we had dug the snow away from one side, he fell over, as he was unable to stand when no longer supported by it. We built a fire to warm the horse. He

bent his legs and stretched them. I gathered some dry grass from the side of the hill and fed him. We also warmed the saddle skin my father had used as a hood and rubbed the horse's legs with it. "Try to rise," my father said to the horse, "and I will make an offering of red cloth that you can wear as a necklace. I will do this as soon as we return to the village." We worked over the horse a long while. Finally, I seized him by the tail while my father held his head and together we raised him to his feet. He fell again and I raised him, whipping him with a stick. He got up weakly. I brought him more grass; he ate anything, biting off even the tops of sticks. I walked him about. My father hunted around and finally spied our other four horses in a bunch in the hills to the north.

When I had tunnelled through the snow my dog met me at the mouth of the tunnel. While we were still in the tent, my father and I heard a noise overhead which we thought made by a ghost, but it was only my dog on the snowdrift above us.

We remained at this spot the rest of that day and through the night, digging the tunnel out to the ground, to reach our tent. We cut the sinews used to sew the skins together and in this way removed the cover, piece by piece. We abandoned the poles.

We set out on our return trip the next day, loading our meat on two of our horses.... The snow was very deep so that we had to stop and camp after we had proceeded about a mile. The following day was quite warm, so we made our way along the tops of hills and rising ground, for the coulees were filled deep with drifted snow....

All our relations now came into our lodge, and my mother cut off pieces of the meat we brought and gave some to each...."

73

MENOMINI HUNTING

"To the present day, no hunter, however skilled, believes for a moment that he could be successful without the aid of sacred charms and incantations," said an ethnologist in 1921 about the Menomini.

When a Menomini boy shot his first animal (or bird), his parents gave what was called the "First Game Feast". The animal was cooked, no matter how small or seemingly worthless, then served to a gathering of tribal leaders who prayed for the young hunter and encouraged him to future success.

Wooden deer calls were used to imitate the sound of a fawn in distress, which generally brought out any doe in the vicinity. Hunters were careful in using this call, however, since it was likely to bring out hungry bears, wolves and wildcats, as well.

In earlier times, group hunts for deer were quite common. Men cut down trees to form two V-shaped parallel rows, sometimes extending through popular feeding areas for several miles. A group of men then fanned out and tried to frighten deer into the larger end of the V, causing them to bunch up at the small end, where several hunters lay concealed.

CHIPPEWA HUNTING CUSTOMS

Moose, deer and bear were the main large animals hunted for food, although the Chippewa ate nearly every kind of bird and animal in their country, including beavers, otters and muskrats.

Before guns were obtained, bow and arrow hunting for large game was often done at night with the use of torches, which were thought to attract the animals, then blind them to the hunters. The most popular torch for this purpose was made from a stick of hazel brush, one end of which was crushed with a stone so that the fibers were separated. This end was then dipped in melted pitch (the gum of any evergreen tree), also used for sealing the joints of birchbark items such as canoes. The pitch-covered stick was then wrapped with a strip of thin cloth, which was coated with more pitch. In place of pitch, tallow from inside the body of a deer was often melted and used the same way. A foot long torch of this kind was said to burn most of the night.

Torch hunting was often done with canoes, the burning stick being held in a socket at the front of the boat. Behind it was placed a shield of bark or board, large enough to keep the flame from shining on the hunter, who stood ready with his weapon right behind.

Deer and moose calls were frequently used to attract these animals, after the hunter concealed himself in a favorable location.

In times of need, hunters painted their faces black and abstained from eating until they found success. Often the wife and children of a hunter in need joined in the fast, which was thought to improve greatly the chances for success.

IN A CHIPPEWA HUNTING CAMP
Told by Nodinens (Little Wind), Age 74

"My home was at Mille Lac, and when the ice froze on the lake we started for the game field. I carried half of the bulrush mats and my mother carried the other half. We rolled the blankets inside the mats; and if there was a little baby, my mother put it inside the roll, cradle board and all. It was a warm place and safe for the baby. I carried a kettle beside my roll of mats. We took only food that was light in weight, such as rice and dried berries, and we always took a bag of dried pumpkin flowers, as they were so nice to thicken the meat gravy during the winter."

"There were six families in our party, and when we found a nice place in the deep woods we made our winter camp. The men shovelled away the snow in a big space, and the six wigwams were put up in a circle and banked with evergreen boughs and snow. Of course, the snow was all shovelled away inside of the wigwam, and plenty of cedar boughs were spread on the ground and covered with blankets for our beds, the bright yarn bags being set along the wall for use as pillows. In the center was a place for a fire, and between it and the floor mats there was a strip of hard, dry ground that was kept clean by sweeping it with a broom made of cedar boughs. The wigwam looked nice with the yellow birch-bark top and the bright-colored things inside. Outside the door there was a little shed made of cedar bark in which we kept the split wood for the fire, so it would not get wet and so we could get it easily in the night. Sometimes there were many of these sheds around the door of a wigwam. The men brought the logs and the women chopped the wood, and put it in the sheds ready for use."

"There was a big fire in the middle of the camp, and all the families did their cooking around this if the weather was not too cold, but we always had a fire in the wigwam in the evening, so it would be warm for us to sleep. We always slept barefoot, with our feet toward the fire, and we loosened our other clothing. I wore a dress of coarse broadcloth, with separate pieces of the cloth to cover my arms, and I had broadcloth leggings that came to my knees, but I wore no other clothing except my moccasins and blanket."

"The big rack for drying meat was over the fire in the middle of the circle. During the day the women kept this fire burning low and evenly to dry the meat. When the men came home at night the rack was taken off the fire, for the men put in lots of light wood to dry their clothing. They sat around it, smoking and talking. If a snowstorm came on we spread sheets of birch-bark over the meat. We did not dry it entirely - only enough so that it would keep - and the drying was finished in the sun when we reached our summer camp."

"The fire blazed brightly until bedtime, and then the men put on dry wood so that it would smoulder all night. The women were busy during the day preparing the meat, attending to their household tasks, and keeping the clothing of the men in order. Each man had two or three leather suits which required considerable mending, as they had such hard wear. We snared rabbits and partridges for food and cleaned and froze all that we did not need at the time."

"The hides were tanned with the hair on and were spread on the cedar boughs along the edge of the wigwam. Father gathered us children around him in the evening and instructed us as we sat on these soft hides. He instructed us to be kind to the poor and aged and to help those who were helpless. This made a deep impression on me, and I have always helped the old people, going into the woods and getting sticks and scraping their kinnikinnick for them."

"During the winter my grandmother made lots of fish nets of nettle-stalk fiber. Everyone was busy. Some of the men started on long hunting trips in the middle of the winter, and did not get back until after the spring work was done; then they rested a while and started off on their fall hunting and trapping."

"Toward the last of the winter my father would say, 'one month after another has gone by. Spring is near and we must get back to our other work.' So the women wrapped the dried meat tightly in tanned deerskins and the men packed their furs on sleds or toboggans. Once there was a fearful snowstorm when we were starting to go back and my father quickly made snowshoes from the branches for all the older people. Grandmother had a supply of thorn-apple thorns and she got these out and pinned up the children's coats so they would be warm and we started off in the snow storm and went to the sugar bush."

(Excerpt from: Densmore, Frances **CHIPPEWA CUSTOMS**)

DEER HUNTING

Deer hunters often used disguises to get near enough for bow and arrow shots. The simplest form of disguise was the head of a buck with the horns left on. The head was carefully skinned, then allowed to dry in its natural shape, after which it was prepared for wearing as a mask.

Navajo hunters followed traditions that required bloodless killing of deer whose heads and skins were to be used as disguises. They were generally run down and smothered. After proper ceremony, the hunter then wore the skin over his head and down his back. He approached feeding deer, preferably in bunches, slowly and from downwind, using brush and tall grass to hide his lower body. Deer can be fooled by their eyes, though rarely by their sense of smell.]The disguised hunter kept his bow and arrows strapped to his und erside, leaving hands free to help him stoop forward. When he was close enough, the hunter ducked behind a bush, fitted his arrow, and possibly got off his first shot without even being noticed. Frequently he was able to get off one or two more shots, as long as he remained downwind and moved slowly.]Lone hunters preferred lying in wait for deer at water springs or mineral licks. If the place was out in the open, he lay concealed nearby and watched which way the animals went afterwards. Deer and others like to visit salt licks or watering holes before they go and bed down. The hunters would follow their tracks very quietly

Because deer are so wary, native hunters preferred to go after them in groups, rather than alone. They would select an area known to have lots of deer, perhaps a meadow, or a small grove of trees. Then part of the group would first approach downwind from the area and take up positions along the main trails, behind boulders, or at the tops of narrow canyons. The other group would then approach the deer from upwind, beating on sticks and shouting to start them running toward the waiting group.

Groups of deer hunters near lakes and rivers would work together to drive the animals from the shoreline into water, where they could be easily shot from behind, or by others waiting on the far side, else by hunters chasing in canoes.

Men generally did all the deer hunting, skinning and carrying home. Women butchered the animals, tanned the hides, and prepared the meat. The custom among many tribes was that once the hunter dropped his animal at the door of the lodge, it belonged to the woman, both to work on and to feed out as she pleased.

MENOMINI BEAR HUNTING

"In olden times, men armed with spears having stone blades and wooden shafts 'a man's height in length', entered bears' dens and slew them single-handed at close quarters. This was considered to be as brave a deed as to slay an enemy.

"Bears were also trapped in various ways. An ancient method still sometimes employed (in 1921) was the deadfall.... This was made of a heavy log, often weighted at the upper end with stones. The log was set up obliquely and was supported by a 'figure 4' trigger. Directly under the log, a small enclosure of stakes was built, in which the bait was placed. In order to get at the lure the bear was obliged to enter the enclosure. The instant that the bait was touched, the trigger to which it was attached released the log, which crashed down on the animal and broke its back...."

"The Ojibwa....utilize a variation of the deadfall for trapping bear, in which the animal, instead of entering an enclosure, is obliged to stretch its neck over a log. When the trigger is released, another log falls crosswise on s0the neck of the brute, and either breaks it or causes death by strangulation."

"Nooses arranged to twitch upward and hang the bear are set in a similar manner.... Bears are also captured in pitfalls.... These are set in the bear path or trail, and covered with rotten sticks or reeds, over which earth and leaves are sprinkled."

"For bait, besides magic lures, honey, apples, pork, beaver musk, and other sweet-smelling or oily substances are used. It is said that a bear will travel a long way out of his path to find the source of any sweet or unusual savor brought to his nostrils by the wind."

"Still hunting on foot with the rifle, or formerly with the bow, was done principally in the late summer, when the bear gorges on raspberries, and travels widely in search of abandoned clearings or burnt-over openings in the forest where the fruit grows in abundance. In the fall the bear roams again, this time feeding principally at night on acorns from the oak trees which cover the sandy plains and ridges. The Indians say that the bear relies on this feast of acorns to provide the fat which is to carry him through his winter sleep. The Menomini declare that at other seasons the bear is met with only by accident, and inhabits the heart of the forest."

"It is said that bears were formerly hunted out in their winter quarters, early in the spring, when the females have just brought forth their young. It was at this time that adventurous youth showed their metal by hand-to-hand conflicts in the den."

SNARING FOR SURVIVAL

Shoelaces, or a piece of nylon fishing line, can be used as an emergency snare if you are lost or injured in the wilderness. Rabbits, squirrels, ducks and grouse are among the easier creatures to capture this way, when the main concern is simply survival.

Make a quarter-inch loop at one end of your snare, then slip the other end through it, leaving an opening according to the size of your quarry. For rabbits, lay this opening along one of their regular trails, then tie the other end to a tree or some brush. Hold the snare open with small sticks or bunches of grass arranged in such a way that the animal must enter the loop in order to go along the trail. Check this setup frequently, at least every morning and night, to make sure nothing suffers for long in it.

A spring-pole setup makes death by snaring go more quickly; it also holds the snared animal out of reach from others who might find it before you. For this method, the snare is attached to the tip of a sapling or small tree. This is bent over and held down by a well-balanced stick to which some bait is attached. When the animal takes the bait, it moves the balanced stick which causes the sapling to spring up, pulling the noose tight and lifting the victim up into the air.

An easy way to snare squirrels is to tie a pole between two trees in an area where many of them live. Smear jam or peanut butter along the top of this pole, if you have any, then place several snare loops so that the squirrels will be caught in them as they run across. Leave a long end on the snare, so that the squirrel will dangle from the pole and not suffer long. Squirrel and rabbit hides were often sewn together in former times to make soft robes and blankets.

Snares along the top of a pole work well to catch some birds, too. Grouse can be tempted with a bit of grain or meal. Make the loops small and fasten them so they don't lie flat; birds will get their feet tangled up in them. For ducks, put the snares on top of a log or board, bait it, then anchor it some distance out in the water.

Prairie chickens, sage hens, grouse and other birds sometimes gather in bunches to feed or hold mating ceremonies. They may dance and chase each other around in a small area each evening for eight or ten days. In former times, young children were taught how to obtain their own food by placing snares in this dance area. One adult bird is enough for a good meal, the skin being easily peeled off while the bird is still warm, removing the feathers with it.

FISHING

It has been said that no other occupation or activity practised by modern humans brings us so close to our Stone Age ancestors as fishing. Although rods, reels, nylon lines and steel hooks are all comparatively recent inventions, their use and purpose is not much different from the hair snares, bone hooks and short harpoons used by ancient fishermen, who had to sit patiently above sites of water just like anglers of today.

Some tribes lived mainly from their fishing, while others hardly touched fish, at all. Among the buffalo-hunting Blackfeet, for instance, fish were considered members of the mystical Underwater Spirits, eaten only in times of near starvation. Most native people caught fish mainly to supplement their hunting.

Fishing lines were made from plant fibers, twisted sinew, the woven hair of horse tails and other natural materials. Coastal people made long lines by knotting together pieces of kelp. Simple hooks were made from bones, else a piece of thorn bush cut so that the thorn formed the point and the stem served as shank. The line was tied to the shank with a piece of sinew, the loose end of which could also serve as bait.

Another hook of sorts was made by sharpening the ends of two short pieces of bird or fish bone. These pieces were then tied together in the shape of a cross, to which was tied a worm, grub or grasshopper. Fish were allowed to swallow the bait before it was jerked up, the cross hopefully stuck somewhere inside its body. In a pinch, bait was sometimes tied to the end of a line without any type of hook. A fish that swallowed it was then gently pulled from the water before it could disgorge the mistake.

Using these primitive lines worked fairly well through holes in Winter ice, or in cases of emergency. But people who ate fish as their main diet could not rely on such haphazard methods. Several kinds of traps were used for obtaining fish in larger quantities. However, there is little purpose in describing the details of these, as their use is now illegal and generally unnecessary.

Fish can be dried and stored just like the meat of animals. The most common way to dry fish is to cut them open lengthwise and spread them apart with sticks. The spread fish are then hung on pole frames by their tails, while fires are kept burning underneath, using brush to create lots of smoke. Cuts are made crosswise on the bodies of larger fish so that air can get into the meat better. Fish only dried on the outside are subject to early rotting. Very large fish are cut up into thin pieces before the drying process, which can take up take up to a week to complete. Each day the fish are rubbed and squeezed by hand to break down the fibers and make them soft. These methods are still practised by the people of several tribes.

Some people preferred to dry their fish in Sunlight, claiming that fire causes them to become stiff, brittle and hard to cook. Also, most of the fat and flavour is said to leave fish hung over fires.

Sun drying was especially used for smaller fish, like trout. Larger fish were often partly dried in the Sun, then hung up indoors to finish.

PACIFIC COAST FISHING

Salmon were so important to some Northwest Coast tribes that their native name for it was the same as for fish, in general. Coastal legends describe salmon as "magic people" who belong to five different tribes, living in longhouses underwater. Catching and eating salmon was a ceremonial act that filled much of their traditional lifestyle. Important tribal rituals followed the catching of each season's first salmon, rituals that were said to have been handed down through the ages since first taught by the magic people themselves.

Salmon were generally prepared with a cut down the backbone, which was removed with the head attached. The rest of the fish was then opened like a book and held that way with short sticks, so that it could be roasted before a fire. Everyone in the tribe took a piece of the first salmon prepared this way, making sure to place all the leftover bones with the back and head, all of which was afterwards thrown back into the water.

Once salmon began their annual run, native people caught them in large quantities, using weirs, dip nets, harpoons and spears. Afterwards, the fish were cleaned and hung up on drying racks by the hundreds, their bones also saved for ceremonial return to the waters.

Dried salmon was the most important food for most Coastal people, as was dried buffalo meat for tribes of the Plains. Properly dried and stored, salmon could be kept for a long time, certainly from one year's salmon run to the next.

To dry salmon, they were again split open as described, except that very large specimens were also sliced into strips. Drying racks were built along the riverbanks or inside the longhouses. Fires were built in rows underneath, the preferred wood being alder. Fish were hung from these racks by their tails, the women watching carefully so that none would burn from being too close, or spoil from being too far away.

It generally takes about a week to smoke dry salmon over a fire. Every day or so, each fish was rubbed and squeezed to soften it, so that the smoke and hot air could get in between all the fibers, otherwise it was more likely to spoil during storage. Outdoors, the drying fish had to be covered in times of rain. At the end, dried salmon were folded up like pieces of cardboard, tied into bundles, then stored in large woven baskets. They were eaten raw, or cooked with other foods such as berries and roots.

MENOMINI ICE FISHING

Holes were chopped into lake ice using a special form of chisel which consisted of a stout wooden handle into which a narrow stone or native-made copper celt was inserted and lashed in such a way as to form one continuous piece. This was then pounded with a stone or wooden club.

Before the arrival of the modern hook and line (which Indian fishermen quickly adopted), bait was not used to catch fish, but only to attract them near enough so they could be speared. The most common bait was an artificial minnow, carved of wood and weighed down with a piece of lead attached to the lure in such a way as to keep it balanced. The lure was tied to a length of cord, then suspended from a short stick, which was jerked so as to produce a lifelike motion.

The fisherman built a small hut of boughs over his hole in the ice, which he covered with a blanket or robe to keep out light, so that he could look far down into the water below.

Net fishermen made a number of holes in the ice, close together, in a long row. Then they dropped their net through the first and largest of these, pushing it along with a pole from one hole to the next, until it was fully strung out. Stone sinkers carried it to the bottom, where fish usually congregate in cold weather.

Winter or summer, fish were eaten fresh after being either boiled or roasted over coals. However, the bulk of a catch was split open and dried, either in the Sun or smoked over an open fire.

Several Menomini delicacies were made from Sturgeon roe, including one in which the roe was kept until the eggs turned black and burst, at which time they are said to have a wonderful taste, in spite of their potent odour.

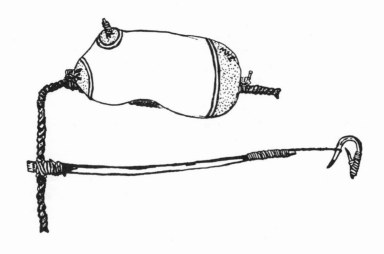

OCEAN FISHING

Certain whaling tribes, like the Makah, Quinault, Haida and Nootka had boats and equipment needed to go after ocean fish that lived far offshore. For this they used a primitive method of deep-sea fishing, including handmade hooks and lines.

Fishing line was often made from kelp, a long stemmed seaweed tough enough to knot together and hold weight without breaking. A heavier rope was made from cedarbark, usually the inner layer of tall, old trees, which was shredded with special tools and then twisted into lengths of rope.

Hooks were generally made from wood, large and sturdy. For instance, a knot of hemlock was carved into a strip about eight inches long and a half inch wide. Sanded smooth, this strip was steamed and bent into a U-shape so that it roughly resembled a horseshoe in size and pattern. Near one end this U-shape was attached to a strip of whale sinew (as a leader), which in turn was fastened to a heavier piece of line, then connected to the long cedarbark rope.

The lower end of the U-shaped hook had a "barb" made from a three-inch piece of sharpened bone, tied on with sinew or a strip of spruce root. For bait, either a small fish, or a piece of wood carved to look like one, was attached so that it moved and caught the fish's attention.

The heavy rope was lowered into deep water with a stone tied at the bottom. The lighter line was tied a bit further up, allowing the wooden hook to float just above the ocean floor. Large halibut, feeding near the bottom, would nose into the U-shaped hook for the bait, then catch themselves on the barb, trying bo back out. Patient fishermen waited in boats above, while those less patient tied their lines to sealskin buoys and waited on shore for movement to indicate that a fish was caught.

SHELLFISH

Among Northwest Coast tribes, fishing was generally men's work, but women gathered shellfish. Most important of these were the half dozen varieties of clam. On some beaches, ancient heaps of clamshells from native eating run along for miles, often several feet deep.

Clams were gathered into special baskets made so that water would drip out the bottom. At home, a pit was lined with rocks, over which a fire was built and allowed to burn down. The clams were placed over the hot stones, then covered with seaweed and allowed to steam, resulting in the popular "clambake", originally a native tradition. Some steamed clams were eaten immediately, the rest were strung on cedar cords and hung up, usually over a fire, until completely dry.

Considered the riskiest food for spoilage unless properly dried, these cedar strings of clams were so popular that they served as standard items of trade, even among interior tribes who did not live along clam beaches. The strings were made with forty butter clams or 12 of the larger horse clams. They were stored in loosely woven baskets that allowed air circulation; they were also turned frequently to keep them from spoiling.

Mussels were pried off rocks at low tide with knives, winter being the favored season. The broken shells were so sharp and strong that they were popular tools before the coming of knives and scissors. Also during low tide, gatherers watched for soft-shelled crabs and marooned fish, which they caught by hand, often clubbing them with wooden sticks first.

STARS, CALENDARS, SEASONS

AND OTHER DIVISIONS OF TIME

Even without clocks and calendars, native people had several ways for keeping track of time and the passing seasons. For instance, the Sun tells you how much of a day has passed, especially when you live outside in its light all day. Certain Stars and their changing positions in the sky tell the passing of night. The changing shape of the Moon indicates how much of the month has passed. For that reason native people always spoke of the months as Moons. Finally, by noting the passing Moons anyone can keep track of the year in progress.

The names and details of seasons varied from region to region, even among families of the same tribe. For those who concerned themselves with thoughts about "new year", that occasion varied from end of Summer, start of Winter of the time of first grass in the Spring. Crop-growing people liked to define four different seasons, while those who lived mainly by hunting concentrated on just two, winter and summer.

Most tribes had certain individuals noted for time keeping, often those in charge of important medicine bundles with annual rituals that had to be carried out at certain times. They would be relied on to know how much longer it was until those times.

For instance, the Keepers of complex Beaver Bundles among the Blackfeet had sets of carved sticks representing days, Moons, even years. As part of their daily requirements to make incense and pray by the bundles, the keeping man and wife also turned one of the sticks, to indicate that another day was gone. At the end of a Moon they turned a different kind of stick, which signified that it was time to gather with other keepers and sing certain so-called Moon Songs.

Individuals wanting to keep track of the days and Moons would tie knots into special thongs, or add beads to it. Others carved notches for Moons and years into the bone handles of their hide scrapers, important tools in primitive life, usually kept near at hand. Some women kept track of time by adding beads to the fringes of their dresses. Such dresses became life-long possessions, worn only on special occasions, sometimes even handed down to children and grandchildren.

Years were recorded not by numbers, like today, but by brief titles outlining the most notable events. Commonly called Winter Counts, they were sometimes recorded on tanned hides, simple figures and drawings illustrating the titles. These drawings usually started in the middle of the hide and slowly spiralled outward. The keeper of such an account might teach its meaning to a younger person, who later inherited the hide and continued it, else kept a copy of his own. Some of the Winter Counts preserved in museum collections go back to the 1700's, listing important battles and peace treaties, solar eclipses, and other events in the skies, starvation and diseases, along with the deaths of chiefs and other notable persons.

Keepers of native calendars kept close watch on events in nature suggesting other important matters, such a storms, droughts and expecta-tions for winters. For instance:

If muskrats built their houses close to shore the people expected a mild Winter. If the houses were some distance from shore they expected an average Winter. However, if muskrats built their houses way out towards the middle of a pond or slough then the people prepared for a tough Winter. Muskrats cannot survive if the water around their houses freezes. In a cold Winter they must be out in deep water to keep from freezing.

If migrating geese flew high it was a sign for a mild Winter. If the geese flew low, people would say: "The geese are close to the ground - we had better look for lots of supplies for the upcoming Winter".

The pelts of animals were checked for their thickness to learn how to prepare for Winter. Of course, one would have to know how thick the pelts normally get.

The colour of rabbits was watched to see how soon Winter would arrive and how soon it would be leaving. Rabbits turn white during Winter.

Winter was expected to come early and strong if curlews stopped singing early in Summer, or if meadowlarks left the area before berries got ripe, or if songbirds were seen gathering in flocks early.

During the Winter, people watched for spectacular Northern Lights, the Aurora Borealis. They said these lights came from the "Woods White Men", who were having a dance in the mysterious Far North. If the lights were bright a big storm could be expected within two days. If the lights were not very bright then a mild storm was expected - often just a lot of wind.

At the end of Winter, people watched gophers digging holes. They said if gophers pile up a lot of dirt outside it means they are digging deep and that the grass would not grow good, that the Buffalo Flowers would not grow tall and the buffalo would not be very fat. Buffalo were said to get good and fat on the Buffalo Flowers.

It is said that "when Sun paints both cheeks" (that is, when two Sun Dogs appear) the weather will turn very bad. When Sun paints "both cheeks", as well as "the forehead and chin" (four Sun Dogs) it is a sign that a great man is going to die.

When a Rainbow shows up during a storm it was said that Thunder was roping the Rain clouds and taking them somewhere else. Then the people knew the storm would soon be over.

Generally speaking, native people considered Spring to start when wild geese were seen heading North. The blooming of wild rose bushes meant Summer was started. Mid-Summer was the time when grass and leaves reached full growth. In the Long Ago many people celebrated Summer Solstice with a mid-Summer ceremony. For instance, the Flatheads had a special place where they gathered to dance each year at that time. Sun Dances are still held at this powerful time. Autumn came with the migrating of birds back toward the South and ended with the leaves turning yellow and falling off.

The time between Moons was referred to by Nights, rather than Days. The four Nights when there is no Moon was called the period of "opening" as when a medicine bundle is being opened to view. Following the opening there are somewhere between twenty-six and thirty nights. These could also be referred to as "Sleeps", like: "We travelled four sleeps to get here."

Some people used a clock of sorts by noting the position of the Sun at certain geographic points or even at certain points along the walls of a tipi. At night the most common way to tell time was by the position of the Big Dipper. The Kootenay People called this the Grizzly Bear. The said the star Polaris is a stake to which the Grizzly Bear was tied to. Each night he revolves around that stake. Day will not begin until the revolution is complete.

The Blackfoot People spoke of the Big Dipper as Seven Brothers who, according to legend, left the earth long ago. In the Old Days a common question of the night was: "How is the last brother pointing?" It meant: "What time is it?" Here is the ancient legend of these Seven Brothers:

Long Ago there was a widowed man who had six grown sons, plus a small son and two daughters, the younger of whom cared for the little boy. To keep the family supplied with food he went out hunting nearly every morning with his six grown sons. As soon as the hunters left each morning, the grown daughter went off to gather firewood.

Time went by and the little girl began to wonder why her older sister always spent so much time gathering firewood and why she went to do it only when the men were away. One day she followed the sister into the brush. There, she was much surprised to see her older sister meeting a large bear and making love with him. She hurried back to their tipi, much confused by what she had seen.

When her father and brothers came home that evening, the young girl waited for a chance to be alone with them so that she could tell about her discovery. The older sister had embarrassed the family several times by turning down good men in the camp who wished her for a wife. The father and brothers were now quite insulted that she should be having an illicit husband who was a bear. They immediately gathered their weapons and went after the bear to kill him.

Afterward, when the bear's sweetheart learned what had happened, she was greatly upset. She went to the body of her lover and took from it a part, which she wrapped up and carried next to her body. Then when the people in the camp learned about the incident they ridiculed the girl until she became very angry. She called on the spirit of her lover for help, after which she turned into a huge bear. She ran through the camp and tore down the lodges, killing most of the people before the power left her and she became herself again. When the younger sister saw what was happening she was greatly frightened. Putting the little brother on her back she ran into the woods to hide. On the trail she encountered her returning brothers, who were in mourning because their father had been killed in an accident while hunting. When they heard what had happened at the camp they were even more grieved. They told their young sister to go back home and secretly gather up spare moccasins and food so that they would be equipped to travel to some distant place together. They told them they would place cactus thorns in front of the tipi door, except for a little path, which she must pass over. That way their older sister could not follow them.

The little sister and brother then returned to the tipis, where she started to gather up the supplies. After a while the older sister realized what was going on, becoming angry again. The little girl quickly put her brother on her back, grabbed the provisions and ran out the door, carefully avoiding the cactus thorns as she ran. The older sister ran after them, but her feet became covered with thorns. As she stood and hollered in pain she again became possessed by her lover's power and turned into a bear. At that she chased after the others.

Now, one of the Brothers had a lot of power of his own. When he saw that the bear was about to catch up, he spit over his shoulders; right away a lake formed behind them. The bear was delayed in going around this water. As she started to catch up again the powerful brother took his porcupine tail brush and threw it behind him. Right away a dense thicket was formed; the bear had a difficult time getting through it. As the bear began to catch up again they decided to climb into a large tree. The bear stood at the bottom and said: "Well, now I will kill you for sure." The powerful brother took out his bow and arrows, as the bear began to shake the tree. Four of the brothers fell out of the branches and were just about to be killed by the bear when an arrow struck between its eyes. Right away the bear turned back into their sister, but now she was dead.

The powerful brother felt sad for having killed his own sister. He said to the others: "Well, we have no one left here on earth, now, so we might as well go somewhere else." The others agreed and asked where they might go. He told them to close their eyes, then he shot an arrow far into the sky. When they opened their eyes back up they were all floating in the sky with him.

In that way was formed the Big Dipper, or Ursa Major. The four brothers who fell from the tree are the four lowest stars in the group, while the other brothers form the remaining three stars. Some say the small star to one side of the Big Dipper's handle is the little sister, while others say that she became married to one of the stars in the Little Dipper, that she is the North Star, or Pole Star. This one is also called "the star that never moves", it served as a night-time compass in the old days.

Another night-time compass was the Morning Star. In legends he is the child of Sun and Moon, which is why he shines during the time between night and day. His arrival on the Eastern horizon always told the people that morning was near. Another star that is not quite so bright comes up before Morning Star and sometimes fooled the people. He was called Mistaken Morning Star. A long legend tells how he became Morning Star's adopted brother, after living on the earth as a young man named Scar-Face.

Morning Star is also known as Jupiter. Mistaken Morning Star is the planet Venus. It was also called the "Day Star", because it can sometimes be seen in the middle of the day. Mars was given the name "Big-Fire Star", because of its red colour. The constellation known today as Lynx was called "Person's Hand". Here is the brief legend behind that name.

Two friends were out hunting buffalo one time, long ago. When they located a small herd they separated so that they would have a better chance of success in case the herd moved away from them. One of the men shot a cow, but the other one got nothing. When he came up to his friend the latter was busy butchering. He said: "Well, friend, I got nothing, so why don't you give me a kidney from your cow?" The other one said: "No, it is not my fault that you scared the herd away - I was lucky to get this one." At that point they began to argue back and forth, with the result that the unsuccessful hunter pushed the other one away and reached in to grab the kidney by himself. With anger the other man slashed his friend's hand off. He, in retaliation, slashed the other's hand off and threw it up into the sky, where it remained to become the Person's Hand. The people then found an organ inside of buffalo which they also called Person's Hand.

NORTHERN INDIAN CALENDAR

People of the Northern Plains and Rockies were hunters whose main seasonal concerns involved Winter and Summer. They considered the "new year" to begin with the trials of Winter, to climax with the mid-Summer celebrations or Sun Dances, and to end after an Autumn of hunting and gathering food supplies.

1. OCTOBER called "When Winter Starts", "First Big Storm", or "When Leaves Fall Off". This latter was the term most commonly used by native tribes to describe this Moon.

2. NOVEMBER also called "When Winter Starts", depending on the weather of that particular year. Also known as the Moon "When Geese Fly South" and "When Big Winds Blow". Among the Kootenay People this was the Moon "When Deer Lament", either because they were mating or because hunters were after them.

3. DECEMBER "When Rivers Freeze", or "When big storm comes and is followed by quiet". A more recent name among tribes such as the Blackfeet is "Big Holy Day Moon", referring to Christmas.

4. JANUARY The Moon "When heavy snows fall". Also called by some the "Helping each other to eat Moon", because the rough weather kept hunters from going out so much and forced the people to share their food supplies. A more recent name is "Kissing Holy Day Moon", for the modern New Year's celebrations.

5. FEBRUARY "More Big Storms", "Eagle Moon", or the "Unpredictable Moon". Those who lived near the Rockies sometimes called it the "Big Chinook Moon". Also called the "Short Moon", because it only stays dark two nights instead of four.

6. MARCH "Geese coming back Moon", also "Time for sore eyes", when the brightness of Sun caused snowblindness. Among the Kootenay, this was the "Snow Melting Moon".

7. APRIL "Ice Breaking Up" and "Long-time Rain Moon". The Kootenays said "Ground Cracking Moon".

8. MAY "Leaves coming out Moon", or "Moon of Last Snow Storm". This storm was particularly dreaded out on the prairies because it often came very suddenly and caught the people by surprise. Also, it tended to drift very deeply, hiding steep cutbanks so that horses and buffalo were likely to fall off them and die. The Flathead People called this the "Bitterroot Moon", when they dug for that important food source.

9. JUNE "Green Grass Moon" and "Moon of High Waters" were among the common names. To the Kootenays this was "When Strawberries Ripen".

10. JULY "Flower Moon" and "Thunder Moon" were two of several common names.

11. AUGUST Most tribes called this the "Berries Ripe Moon". Among the Blackfeet it was also the "Moon of the Medicine Lodge", when they generally held their annual Sun Dance ceremonies.

12. SEPTEMBER "Moon when leaves fall", "Long-time Rain Moon", or simply "End of Summer Moon" were among the common names.

YUMA INDIAN CALENDAR
from Juan Chicken

The beginning of a new year varied among the desert tribes of the lower Colorado River region, even among families within those tribes. The Cocopa felt this time came when the first heavy frosts killed vegetation, which was usually in early December. Many Yuma considered a year to run from one budding of mesquite and willow to the next. Other people said their new year started with the building of annual winter homes, in the Fall.

All these tribes recognized the same basic four seasons that modern people still use. Spring was from the time the cottonwoods began budding to the time of high water (which varied from year to year). Summer began with high water and ended with it low, usually around September. Autumn was the time of dropping temperatures, usually ending sometime in No-vember, after which came the cold of Winter. A month was called a "Moon", running from the dark of one Moon to the next.

1. First Moon Late February, early March. "When leaves of Cotton wood trees begin to bud". Little activity at this time.

2. Second Moon March "When mesquite and willow begin to bud". Also called the "Windy Moon". New land was cleared for planting; first important efforts at hunting.

3. Third Moon April "Planting Moon", more land clearing; lots of hunting and fishing. First planting after river began to flood.

4. Fourth Moon Late April, early May. "Wild Berry Moon", busy time for fishing and gathering of berries.

5. Fifth Moon Late May and June. "High Water Moon". Period of scarce food, before crops ripen. While fish were hard to find in high water. Fish stranded in shallow waters were shot. Bulk of planting done near end of this Moon.

6. Sixth Moon Late June, early July. "Mesquite Moon", important gathering of mesquite pods and pigweed greens to provide fresh food. Last of planting.

7. Seventh Moon Late July, most of August. "Hoeing Moon". Wild screwbeans harvested; also many fish from river.

8. Eighth Moon September. "Corn Moon". Harvesting of green corn, pigweed greens, pinyon nuts, many river fish.

9. Ninth Moon Late October, November. "Harvest Moon". Garden crops harvested; important dances and ceremonies; much hunting for rabbits and birds.

10. Tenth Moon November. "Frost Moon". Building of winter homes, last harvests.

11. Eleventh Moon December. "Mid-Winter Moon". Not much activity; some bird and rabbit hunting.

12. Twelfth Moon January, early February. "Dried Cane Moon". Not much activity; food scarce; rabbits and birds sought.

CHIPPEWA CALENDAR

1. January "Big Spirit Moon".
2. February "Snow-crusted Moon".
3. March "Broken Snowshoe Moon" (Crusted snow at this time frequently caused snowshoe webbing to break).
4. April "Maple Sugar Making Moon".
5. May "Flower Moon".
6. June "Strawberry Moon".
7. July "Berry Moon".
8. August "Rice Moon".
9. September "Shining Leaf Moon".
10. October "Cold Wind Moon".
11. November "Freezing Moon".
12. December "Small Spirit Moon".

BIBLIOGRAPHY

Castetter, Edward F. and Willis H. Bell
YUMAN INDIAN AGRICULTURE; University of New Mexico Press, 1951.
Cushing, Frank Hamilton
ZUNI BREADSTUFF; Museum of the American Indian, Heye Foundation, New York, 1920.
Densmore, Frances **CHIPPEWA CUSTOMS;** Bulletin 86, Smithsonian Institution, Bureau of American Ethnologhy, 1929.
Dore, William G. **WILD RICE;** Publication 1393, Research Branch, Canada Department of Agriculture, Ottawa.
Hungry Wolf, Adolf **THE BLOOD PEOPLE;** Harper & Row, New York, 1977.
Krober, Theodora **ISHI IN TWO WORLDS;** University of California, Berkeley, 1961
Skinner, Alanson Material **CULTURE OF THE MENOMINI,** Museum of the American Indian, Heye Foundation, New York, 1921.
Stubbs, Ron **Thesis on Flathead Plants, Montana State University.**
Teit, James A. **ETHNOBOTANY OF THE THOMPSON INDIANS OF BRITISH COLUMBIA,** 45th Annual Report of the Bureau of American Ethnology, 1928.
Underhill, Ruth **INDIANS OF THE PACIFIC NORTHWEST,** U.S. Department of the Interior, BIA Branch of Education, 1945.
Underhill, Ruth **HERE COME THE NAVAHO!,** U.S. Department of the Interior, BIA Branch of Education, 1953.
Weltfish, Gene **THE LOST UNIVERSE**
Wilson, Gilbert Livingstone AGRICULTURE OF THE HIDATSA INDIANS, Bulletin of the University of Minnesota No. 9, 1917.
Wilson, Gilbert Livingstone **THE HORSE AND DOG IN HIDATSA CULTURE,** Anthropological Papers, American Museum of Natural History, vol. 15, pt. 2, 1924.